COUNTRY HARVEST

COUNTRY HARVEST

Over 175 recipes for jams, chutneys,
breads and cakes with ideas for
drying and arranging flowers

Linda Burgess and Rosamond Richardson

GUILD PUBLISHING

LONDON · NEW YORK · SYDNEY · TORONTO

This edition published 1990 by Guild Publishing
by arrangement with Ebury Press
an imprint of the Random Century Group
Random Century House
20 Vauxhall Bridge Road
London SW1V 2SA

Editor: Alison Wormleighton
Recipe editor: Barbara Croxford
Designer: Bob Hook
Home economist: Meg Jansz

CN 4547

Filmset in Garamond by Advanced Filmsetters (Glasgow) Ltd
Printed and bound in Italy by New Interlitho S.p.a., Milan

NOTES ON THE PLANTS

When collecting material from the countryside, never
pick endangered species. Lists of plants that it is illegal
to pick, in whole or in part, are available from local
libraries, natural history societies and some wildflower
guidebooks.
Certain sites with fragile or unusual ecologies are
protected in their entirety, so that in those places even
common plants cannot be dug up.
If you take flowers at the seed stage, shake some seeds on
to the ground (except for colonizers like dock).
Remember that you need the landowner's permission to
enter his property and to take his plants.

NOTES ON THE RECIPES

All measurements give the metric amount first, followed
in brackets by the Imperial equivalent, and then the U.S.
equivalents if different. As these are not exact
equivalents, please work from one set of figures. U.S.
teaspoons, tablespoons, pints, quarts and gallons are all
smaller than Imperial ones.
If you cannot find U.S. self-rising flour, use all-
purpose flour plus ¼ teaspoon U.S. baking powder for
each cup of flour.
If you cannot find crème fraîche, a good substitute is two
parts heavy cream mixed with one part sour cream.
Similarly, sour cream may be substituted for fromage
frais if it is unavailable.

CONTENTS

CHAPTER ONE

Jams, Jellies, Chutneys and Conserves

High summer wanes. September comes and the last of the farmer's harvest is being reaped. Combine-harvesters roar over the wheatfields; a light wind chases clouds across the blueness of a wide sky. As the day dwindles a low sun highlights the pale gold stubble. A row of wheat stands uncut, dun-coloured in the oblique light, ready to be harvested at daybreak.

Grasses on the field verges are losing their summer colour. Tall hogweed stands proud against the skyline alongside wispy rosebay willowherb, whiskery white. In the hedgerow nearby a cluster of guelder-rose berries startles with its bright scarlet, and the first wine-black elderberries hang heavy on slender branches.

The gardener begins to reap the fruits of his spring and summer labours as September ticks by, watching the ripening harvest of tomatoes, marrows, pumpkins, beans and carrots. He looks to his crop of fruit trees – pear and plum, apple and quince, mulberries even and greengages – and bides his time to gather them at their peak of ripeness. In sunny sheltered spots the fig tree bears its luscious fruit. The bounty of the land in abundance.

Beyond the garden, in the lanes that lead through the fields and meadows, there is another harvest, a wild harvest traditionally gathered by country people over the centuries. Blackberries are beginning to ripen, with that distinctive flavour which epitomizes autumn. Bright orange rowan berries hang in clusters from slender branches, ready for jelly-making. Elderberries and crab apples, almost always plentiful, are ready to be gathered for jams and conserves, pies and puddings. The bluish-purple damson begins to swell, and its cousin the golden bullace is starting to turn colour. The rare medlar erupts with its bizarre, brown fruits. Lavender is ready to be harvested and hung up in bunches to dry.

It is the season of preserving, of gathering in the harvest both cultivated and wild, to make jellies and chutneys and jams so as to enjoy these flavours over the barren months of winter. By then the trees will be leafless, the last of the berries foraged by birds and small wintering mammals. So the kitchen becomes a hive of activity: the preserving pan is brought out from its annual retirement, jam jars collected and washed ready for use, the larder cleared for this year's harvest. The store cupboard is to be lined with pots of all shapes and sizes, containers of wonderful preserves. The greyness of winter will be transformed by this carnival of tastes, colours and textures to be enjoyed to the full.

RIGHT: MARROW OR SQUASH AND PINEAPPLE JAM (PAGE 32), GREENGAGE JAM (PAGE 26), PEARS IN RED WINE (PAGE 45), PEAR AND WALNUT JAM (PAGE 43)

Preserving is one area of cooking that has changed very little over the centuries. The traditional methods employed by country folk are still in use today for making jams, jellies, chutneys and conserves of all kinds.

Jams

Jam-making, like other forms of preserving, is largely a matter of common sense, and the basic techniques are very straightforward.

INGREDIENTS AND EQUIPMENT
You need very little specialized equipment for making jam, but you do need top-quality ingredients.

Fruit
Choose firm, ripe fruit, always fresh and of good quality. Never use over-ripe fruit, because the jam will not set – the pectin in it is changing to pectin acid. In a wet season, fruit has a lower sugar content than normal, so there is an increased tendency to mildew and less likelihood of it keeping for a long time. Always wash or rinse the fruit before using it, to remove any traces of dust or dirt. Remove all stalks from the fruits, and hull them.

Sugar
Use lump sugar (sugar cubes), preserving sugar or granulated sugar – in that order of preference. Avoid the dark sugars since they change the colour of the fruit and mask its flavour. Sugar is vital for the setting process, and the necessary proportion is 55–70 per cent. If you warm the sugar slightly before stirring it in, it will dissolve more quickly. Do not use too much sugar, or your jam could crystallize during storage.

Preserving pans
Use a preserving pan which is easily large enough – it should not be more than half-full when the fruit and sugar are added, or the jam will boil over when it is at a rolling boil. For best results,

choose a heavy-bottomed aluminium or stainless steel pan – never use iron or zinc pans since the acid in the fruit will attack the metal, and the colour and flavour of the jam will be destroyed. Enamel pans do not conduct heat fast enough for satisfactory jam-making, and tend to burn easily. Tin may melt. You can use a copper pan if you like, but be sure to remove all traces of polish before cooking the fruit, and bear in mind that much of the vitamin C content of the fruit will be destroyed by its reaction with the metal.

Other equipment
wooden spoons – preferably long-handled
large nylon or hair sieve
slotted spoon
sharp stainless-steel knives
serrated knife
chopping board
juice squeezer
food-processor with mincer blades (useful but not essential)
wide-lipped jug for pouring
funnel
jam thermometer
plastic screw-top jam jars
waxed and cellophane discs
labels

TESTING FOR SET
Test for set when the jam begins to thicken, using one of the following methods. Broadly speaking, the stage of boiling the jam to setting point takes about 10 minutes. Avoid over-boiling. It spoils the colour and flavour and prevents the jam from keeping very long.

If the jam should fail to set, add 30 ml (2 tbsp) lemon juice per 1.8 kg (4 lb) fruit and try again – or add commercial pectin in the quantity recommended on the label.

Flake test
When the jam begins to thicken, dip in a wooden spoon and hold it over the pan. If, as the jam drops off the spoon, it forms a sheet and drops

off as cleanly as a flake, then the jam will set when cold.

Saucer test

When the jam starts to thicken, drop a teaspoonful of the mixture on to a cold saucer and put in a cold place. Draw the pan of jam off the heat. Wait for 5 minutes, then tilt the saucer. If the jam wrinkles a little and does not run, it is ready for potting. If it is still liquid and runs over the saucer, return the jam to the heat and continue boiling it until the test is successful. Be sure to test every few minutes to avoid over-boiling.

Thermometer test

You will need a reliable cook's thermometer which goes up to and includes 104°C/220°F. Always put a thermometer into hot water before you lower it into the jam, to prevent it from cracking. To test for set, stir the jam so that the temperature is even throughout, and when the thermometer reads 104°C/220°F a good set should be obtained. In some cases a reading one degree higher will be better.

THE FINAL TOUCH

A knob of butter added just before the end of the cooking time gives the jam a shine, and also makes scum easier to remove since it causes it to collect in one place. Lift the scum off with a metal spoon and discard. If there are any more traces of scum, these are easily removed by dipping absorbent kitchen paper on to them and lifting them off. A good jam will be firm in set without being solid. It will be clear rather than cloudy, and it will have a fresh fruit flavour.

POTTING AND COVERING

Choose suitably sized jam jars with plastic screw-tops (metals ones corrode). Wash and rinse them thoroughly in hot water. Dry them, and then keep the jars warm until ready for use. Pour or ladle the jam into a jar up to the neck. Cover immediately with a waxed disc, waxed side down,

to keep any dust out. Leave to cool, then place a cellophane disc over the top of the jar and screw the plastic top down over it. Wipe the jars clean. Label clearly, with the date as well as the contents.

STORAGE

Store in a cool, dark, dry place. Heat will shrink the contents of the jar, light will fade the colour of the jam, and damp will encourage mould.

If your jam should crystallize during storage, this is due to either using too much sugar, or over-boiling. It may also happen when the storage place is too dry. You can remedy this by re-heating the jam gently to nearly boiling point and then repotting. The jam will, however, go sugary again in time.

Jellies

Like jam-making, jelly-making is very simple. However, jelly takes longer than jam because the juice has to be strained.

THE JELLY BAG

In addition to the basic equipment needed for jam-making, you will need a jelly bag or a clean linen cloth for straining the juice from the cooked fruit. Cleanliness is paramount at this stage: always scald the cloth or jelly bag in boiling water before use, then wring it dry.

The traditional way to suspend a jelly bag or cloth is to use an upturned kitchen chair. To do this, tie the suspending tapes of the jelly bag, or the four corners of the linen cloth, to the four legs. Make sure that you have tied them very securely — the weight of the fruit and water is considerable. Place a bowl underneath and allow the juice to drip through, undisturbed, for several hours or overnight. Do not squeeze the bag in order to extract the maximum juice, or the jelly will turn cloudy.

BASIC METHOD

Make sure that the fruit you are using is clean. Discard any fruit that is mouldy or over-ripe. It is best to pick the fruit on a dry day, because wet fruit attracts mildew. Rinse it to remove any dirt or grit.

The juice of the cooked fruit is strained through the scalded jelly bag or linen cloth, and measured. The general rule for jellies is to add 450 g (1 lb/2 cups) sugar to every 600 ml (1 pint/2½ cups) juice. This gives a jelly which will both set and keep, although the ratio varies slightly in recipes for different fruits. About 4.5 kg (10 lb) jelly will result from every 2.7 kg (6 lb) sugar used.

Stir over a medium heat until the sugar has dissolved, then bring to the boil and boil fast to setting point. This will take about 10 minutes, or longer if the fruit has a high water content. The methods of testing for set are the same as for jams (see page 10).

Skim the jelly with a metal spoon and remove the last traces of scum with a piece of absorbent kitchen paper. Pour immediately into warm, clean jars, before it has a chance to set in the pan. Cover each jar at once with a waxed disc, waxed side down, and then with a cellophane disc. You can do this when it is either hot or cold. Be careful not to tilt the jars until the jelly has set. Store in a cool, dry, dark place.

Chutney

Making chutney is even easier than making jam or jelly because you do not have to worry about setting or about straining it.

INGREDIENTS AND EQUIPMENT

Use fresh fruit or vegetables which are not over-ripe or damaged. Prepare them as instructed in the recipe, and put them into an aluminium pan. (Metal such as brass, copper or iron will react with the acid in the vinegar and spoil both the pan and the chutney.)

Use the best quality vinegar you can — it will add greatly to the flavour of the chutney or preserve. White vinegar shows off the colour and texture of a pickle better than a dark one. Malt vinegar is used mainly in dark fruit and vegetable chutneys.

BASIC METHOD

Long, steady cooking is required for a good chutney; it should not be over-boiled. The chutney is ready as soon as the mixture thickens to the point where pools of vinegar no longer collect on the surface.

Allow the cooked chutney to cool for a while in the preserving pan before bottling, because it shrinks considerably as it loses heat. Pot in clean jars while still tepid, prodding out any air bubbles from the mixture and making sure that the chutney is well packed down. Cover with waxed discs and put on an outer cellophane disc. Screw down with plastic screw-tops — metal ones will rust and corrode. Wipe the jars clean with a damp cloth, then label when dry. Store in a cool, dark, dry place. Allow them to mature for at least a month before using. Chutneys improve greatly with maturity, and some will keep for many years.

Mulberry Jelly

This beautiful, dark, purplish-red jelly has all the excellent flavour of that luscious fruit, the mulberry. Beware, however, the gathering process — mulberries stain horribly, dripping masses of purple juice even as you stand under the tree. Wear your oldest clothing for this expedition!

2.7 kg (6 lb) mulberries (not too ripe)
juice of 2 lemons
sugar

Put the mulberries, lemon juice and water to cover in a preserving pan. Simmer for about 2 hours or until the juice is drawn out and the fruit pulpy. Strain through a jelly bag for several hours.

Measure the juice into the cleaned preserving pan. To every 600 ml (1 pint/2½ cups) juice, add 350 g (12 oz/1½ cups) sugar. Stir over a gentle heat until the sugar has dissolved. Bring to the boil and boil until setting point is reached.

Pour the jelly into warm, clean jars and cover. Seal.
Makes 3.2 kg (7 lb)

Mulberry Preserve

In the garden of our house when I was a child, we had an ancient mulberry tree. I remember its gnarled trunk and twisted branches, and the huge, floppy, slightly rough leaves. The mulberries were enormous, first bright red, then turning almost purple. They made a scrumptious preserve which I recall eating on freshly baked bread sitting by the kitchen range.

1.8 kg (4 lb) mulberries
150 ml (¼ pint/⅔ cup) water
1.4 kg (3 lb/6 cups) sugar

Put the mulberries into a preserving pan with the water. Simmer gently for 10 minutes until the mulberries are soft. Add the sugar and stir until dissolved. Bring to the boil and boil rapidly until setting point is reached.

Pot the preserve in warm, clean jars and cover. Seal when cold.
Makes 2.3 kg (5 lb)

Brandied Cranberries

The tart flavour of the bright scarlet cranberry goes very well with rich meats and has a special affinity with orange. Preserved with brandy and orange-flavoured liqueur, cranberries make a luxury addition to a buffet table. Attractively bottled, they are also an original Christmas gift.

450 g (1 lb) cranberries
450 g (1 lb/2 cups) sugar
grated rind of 1 orange
150 ml (¼ pint/⅔ cup) brandy and
orange-flavoured liqueur, mixed

Put the cranberries, sugar, orange rind and brandy mixture into a large, shallow, ovenproof dish. Mix well. Leave to stand for 30 minutes. Cover the dish with foil.

Cook in the oven at 170°C/325°F/mark 3 for 30 minutes. Cool slightly.

Pot the preserve in warm, clean jars and cover. Seal. Store in a cool place.
Makes 900 g (2 lb)

Green and black fingers of the trees, dividing
And reaching out towards an otherwhere,
Threaded with birds and birds' sweet sudden gliding,
Pattern and jargoning of tree-tops, such a world
Tangled and resonant and earth-deriding,
Now with the rain-drops' rounded globes bepearled,
And little sullen moons of mistletoe,
Now fretted with the sun, when foxes play
At fables on the dun and foxlike ground
Between the tree-trunks, and the squirrels go
Scuttering with a beechnut newly found,
To vex the pigeon and to scare the jay.

Vita Sackville-West: 'The Land'

The mulberry tree is a symbol of prudence: not a leaf appears on its branches until all danger of frost is over and past.

ROWAN JELLY (PAGE 16), PEAR AND ROSEMARY JELLY (PAGE 44), MINT JELLY (PAGE 19), FRENCH QUINCE JELLY (PAGE 52), GREEN GRAPE JELLY (PAGE 35)

Cranberry and Orange Conserve

Cranberry sauce in one form or another is a must at Christmas and Thanksgiving – the festivities would not be the same without it. There are variations on the theme, of course, and this one, with orange, has the added texture of raisins and walnuts.

2 oranges, peeled
450 g (1 lb) cranberries
300 ml (½ pint/1¼ cups) water
50 g (2 oz/⅓ cup) raisins
50 g (2 oz/½ cup) walnuts, coarsely chopped
350 g (12 oz/1½ cups) sugar

Finely slice the oranges, discarding the pips. Cut the slices into quarters. Put them into a preserving pan with the cranberries and water. Simmer for about 15–20 minutes until tender.

Add the raisins, walnuts and sugar. Stir over a gentle heat until the sugar has dissolved. Bring to the boil and boil rapidly for about 10 minutes, stirring occasionally, or until setting point is reached.

Pot the conserve in warm, clean jars and cover. Seal when cold.
Makes 900 g (2 lb)

Cranberry Wine Jelly

The strong flavours in this recipe – the tart freshness of cranberries mingling with red wine – make an excellent jelly to go with equally strong-flavoured food. It comes into its own at Christmas for meals both hot and cold.

900 g (2 lb) cranberries
300 ml (½ pint/1¼ cups) water
sugar
300 ml (½ pint/1¼ cups) red wine

Put the cranberries into a preserving pan with the water. Cover and simmer gently for about 25 minutes until tender. Strain through a jelly bag for several hours or overnight.

Measure the juice into the cleaned preserving pan. To every 600 ml (1 pint/2½ cups) juice, add 350 g (12 oz/1½ cups) sugar. Stir over a gentle heat until the sugar has dissolved. Add the wine. Bring to the boil and boil rapidly for about 10 minutes, stirring occasionally, or until setting point is reached.

Skim, pour the jelly into warm, clean jars and cover. Seal immediately.
Makes 1.4 kg (3 lb)

Rowan Jelly

The rowan or mountain ash is a delightful tree – very delicate in structure and leaf shape, with clusters of bright orange-red berries in late summer. There are actually several species of European and American mountain ash, or rowan. They are usually the first fruits to appear in the autumn hedgerow, and every year I make this superb jelly. Sharp, with a unique flavour, it is fantastic with all kinds of foods – chicken, cheeses, roast meats – or simply spread on toast. This jelly also has a most beautiful colour.

1.8 kg (4 lb) rowan berries, stripped off stalks
30 ml (2 tbsp/3 tbsp) lemon juice
sugar

Put the berries into a preserving pan with water to cover. Simmer for about 15–20 minutes until soft. Add the lemon juice. Strain through a jelly bag for several hours or overnight.

Measure the juice into the cleaned preserving pan. To every 600 ml (1 pint/2½ cups) juice, add 350 g (12 oz/1½ cups) sugar. Stir over a gentle heat until the sugar has dissolved. Bring to the boil and boil rapidly until setting point is reached.

Cool slightly, then pour the jelly into warm, clean jars and cover. Seal when cold. Store in a cool dark place.
Makes 2.3 kg (5 lb)

Farmers used to make plough-handles with rowan wood to cast evil spirits off the land, and also to bring luck to the person using them. If you place a rowan twig in your pocket it will shield you from the evil thoughts of others. Rowan twigs intertwined in a thatched roof are supposed to prevent the house from catching fire.

CRANBERRY AND ORANGE CONSERVE (THIS PAGE)

Berries in Muscat Wine

This is one of the prettiest of late summer preserves, using as many of the berries as I can find – even if I have to buy rather than gather the blueberries! The multicoloured mixture looks beautiful in large storage jars, gleaming in a syrup made from sweet, golden muscat wine – a kind of autumn fruit salad with a difference. I like to serve the berries with crème fraîche or thick, creamy Greek yogurt, and the Cob Nut (Filbert) Cookies on page 78.

ripe berries, such as blackberries, late raspberries, blueberries, elderberries, mulberries, cranberries

sugar

muscat wine

Hull or stalk the berries, then weigh them. To every 450 g (1 lb) fruit, use 225 g (8 oz/1 cup) sugar.

Pack the berries into clean jars, sprinkling the layers with sugar as you pack.

When the fruit reaches the neck of the jar, fill up with the wine.

Cover and seal.

Store in a cool place.

Mint Jelly

This classic jelly is the ideal complement to roast lamb, counteracting its richness perfectly.

2.3 kg (5 lb) cooking apples (tart green apples), chopped
1.1 litres (2 pints/5 cups) water
4 sprigs fresh mint
300 ml ($\frac{1}{2}$ pint/1$\frac{1}{4}$ cups) white vinegar
sugar
90–120 ml (6–8 tbsp/$\frac{1}{2}$–$\frac{2}{3}$ cup) finely chopped mint

Place apples in a large saucepan with the water and mint. Bring to the boil and simmer gently for 45 minutes till soft and pulpy, stirring occasionally. Add the vinegar and boil for 5 minutes.

Strain through a jelly bag overnight. Measure the juices and put in a preserving pan with 450 g/1 lb sugar for each 600 ml (1 pint/2$\frac{1}{2}$ cups) juice. Stir over a gentle heat until the sugar has dissolved, then boil rapidly for about 10 minutes until setting point is reached.

Remove the pan from the heat and skim off any scum with a slotted spoon. Stir in the chopped mint.

Allow to cool slightly, then stir the jelly. Pour into warm, clean jars and cover. Seal immediately.
Makes about 3 kg (6$\frac{1}{2}$ lb).

Bilberry or Blueberry Conserve

You can use either wild bilberries for this conserve, or the commercially available blueberries, which are slightly larger, sweeter and bluer.

1.1 kg (2$\frac{1}{2}$ lb) bilberries or blueberries
150 ml ($\frac{1}{4}$ pint/$\frac{2}{3}$ cup) water
45 ml (3 tbsp/4 tbsp) lemon juice
1.4 kg (3 lb/6 cups) sugar
knob of butter
225 ml (8 fl oz/1 cup) pectin

Put the bilberries or blueberries into a preserving pan with the water and lemon juice. Simmer gently for 10–15 minutes until the fruit is soft and just beginning to pulp. Remove the pan from the heat, add the sugar and stir until dissolved. Add the knob of butter.

Bring to the boil and boil rapidly for 3 minutes. Remove from the heat and add the pectin. Return to the heat and boil until setting point is reached.

Cool slightly, then pot the conserve in warm, clean jars and cover. Seal while still hot.
Makes about 2.3 kg (5 lb)

Elderberry and Crab Apple Chutney

This chutney matures well – you can keep it for several years and it improves all the time, so long as it is kept well-sealed.

225 g (8 oz/2 cups) onions, skinned and minced
600 ml (1 pint/2$\frac{1}{2}$ cups) vinegar
700 g (1$\frac{1}{2}$ lb) elderberries, stripped off stalks
700 g (1$\frac{1}{2}$ lb) crab apples, cored and sliced
225 g (8 oz/1$\frac{1}{3}$ cups) sultanas (golden raisins)
5 ml (1 tsp) ground ginger
5 ml (1 tsp) ground allspice
5 ml (1 tsp) ground cinnamon
5 ml (1 tsp) cayenne
100 g (4 oz/$\frac{1}{2}$ cup) salt
225 g (8 oz/1 cup) sugar

Put the onions with water to cover in an aluminium preserving pan. Simmer for about 5 minutes until tender. Strain and add a third of the vinegar and all the other ingredients, except the sugar. Simmer until all the elderberry juices are drawn out and the mixture thickens.

Add a second third of the vinegar and simmer again until thick. Add the rest of the vinegar, and the sugar, and simmer until thick, and no liquid is visible when a wooden spoon is drawn through the mixture.

Pack the chutney in warm, clean jars and cover. Seal.
Makes 2.7 kg (6 lb)

Spiced Hedgerow Jelly

This jelly makes the most of the hedgerow harvest over the few weeks when the hedgerows are laden with fruits and berries. It has a true country flavour – strong and definitive, and uncompromisingly natural.

2.3 kg (5 lb) fruit, such as elderberries, stripped off their stalks; blackberries, hulled; crab apples, cored and chopped; damsons, stoned and halved
450 ml ($\frac{3}{4}$ pint/2 cups) water
5 cm (2 inch) piece of fresh root ginger
4 cloves
7.5 cm (3 inch) cinnamon stick

Put the fruits into a preserving pan with the water. Simmer for 30 minutes. Cool a little, then strain through a jelly bag for several hours or overnight.

Measure the juice into the cleaned preserving pan. To every 600 ml (1 pint/2$\frac{1}{2}$ cups) juice, add 450 g (1 lb/2 cups) sugar. Tie the spices in a muslin (cheesecloth) bag and add to the pan. Stir over a gentle heat until the sugar has dissolved. Bring to the boil and boil until setting point is reached. Remove the bag of spices.

Pour the jelly into warm, clean jars and cover. Seal.
Makes 3.2 kg (7 lb)

Japonica (Japanese Quince) and Blackberry Jelly

I have a small japonica bush near my kitchen window, with apricot-coloured flowers in spring and pale golden-yellow fruits, which look rather like miniature knobbly quinces, in the autumn. Combining these with blackberries makes a beautiful jelly with a special fragrance.

450 g (1 lb) japonica (Japanese quince) fruits
900 g (2 lb) blackberries
sugar

Put the japonica (Japanese quince) fruits with water to cover in a preserving pan and simmer for about 30 minutes until soft. Add the blackberries for the last 15 minutes of the cooking time. Strain through a jelly bag overnight.

Measure the juice into the cleaned preserving pan. To every 600 ml (1 pint/2$\frac{1}{2}$ cups) juice add 450 g (1 lb/2 cups) sugar. Stir over a medium heat until the sugar has dissolved. Bring to the boil and boil until setting point is reached.

Pour the jelly into warm, clean jars and cover. Seal.
Makes 1.8 kg (4 lb)

Blackberry Jelly

This jelly is a must. Blackberries make one of the very best jellies in the world. In this recipe, I have included a cooking apple to enhance the flavour of the berries, but if you prefer you can substitute its weight for more berries. An old country trick is to include some red berries along with the ripe ones – they fortify the flavour significantly. Delicious with the Quick Poppy Seed Loaf, still warm from the oven (see page 68).

900 g (2 lb) blackberries, hulled
1 large cooking apple (tart green apple), chopped
150 ml ($\frac{1}{4}$ pint/$\frac{2}{3}$ cup) water
sugar

Put the blackberries and apple into a preserving pan with the water. Simmer very gently for 20–25 minutes until the fruit is very soft. Strain through a jelly bag for several hours or overnight.

Measure the juice into the cleaned preserving pan. To every 600 ml (1 pint/2$\frac{1}{2}$ cups) juice, add 450 g (1 lb/2 cups) sugar. Stir over a gentle heat until the sugar has dissolved. Bring to the boil and boil rapidly for about 10 minutes or until setting point is reached.

Skim if necessary, then pour the jelly into warm, clean jars and cover. Seal immediately.
Makes 1.8 kg (4 lb)

Blackberries must not be gathered after October 11th, according to an old country tradition. October 11th was the old Michaelmas Day, before the calendar changes of 1752. It was on this day that Satan was thrown out of heaven by the Archangel Michael. He fell into a bramble bush, and now every year he takes his revenge by spitting and urinating on the blackberry plant on the anniversary of his disgrace. Not only, it is said, will the berries taste sour, but they will bring you bad luck. In any case, by this time of year the fruit is usually past its best – it is beginning to shrivel and is often infested with insects. So the blackberry harvest is best gathered well before the middle of October. Hence the country saying: 'October's blackberries are the Devil's.'

Hedgerow Jam

At the peak of the autumn harvest, when the hedgerows are laden with berries and nuts of all kinds, it is immensely satisfying to gather a selection for this superb autumnal jam.

450 g (1 lb) elderberries stripped off their stalks
450 g (1 lb) crab apples, cored and sliced
450 g (1 lb) blackberries, hulled
450 g (1 lb) wild plums, stoned and chopped
1.7 litres (3 pints/7½ cups) water
2.3 kg (5 lb/10 cups) sugar
225 g (8 oz/2 cups) hazelnuts (filberts), coarsely chopped
100 g (4 oz/1 cup) walnuts, coarsely chopped

Put all the fruit into a preserving pan with the water. Simmer for 15 minutes.

Add the sugar and stir over a moderate heat until dissolved. Bring to the boil and boil rapidly. After 5 minutes, add the nuts and continue boiling for about 10 minutes, stirring occasionally, or until setting point is reached.

Skim if necessary, then pot the jam in warm, clean jars and cover. Seal while still hot.
Makes 3.6 kg (8 lb)

JUG OF MULBERRY JELLY (PAGE 14), BLACKBERRY AND APPLE JAM (PAGE 22), APPLE, PEAR AND PLUM JAM (PAGE 25)

Pickled Blackberries

Pickled blackberries are a great favourite of mine. The sweet, succulent berries lend themselves well to being pickled in a spiced vinegar. They are a regular part of a simple lunch for my family, or a buffet table of winter salads.

450 g (1 lb/2 cups) sugar (preferably loaf sugar)
300 ml (½ pint/1¼ cups) vinegar
5 ml (1 tsp) allspice berries
5 ml (1 tsp) cloves
two 7.5 cm (3 inch) cinnamon sticks
900 g (2 lb) blackberries, hulled

Put the sugar and vinegar in an aluminium preserving pan. Stir over a gentle heat until the sugar has dissolved. Tie the spices in a muslin (cheesecloth) bag. Add to the pan and simmer for several minutes. Add the blackberries and cook for 10–15 minutes. Remove the bag of spices.

Pack the blackberries into hot, clean jars. Boil the vinegar hard until it turns syrupy. Cover the blackberries with the vinegar, then seal.
Makes 1.8 kg (4 lb)

Blackberry and Apple Jam

This classic jam, featuring that unbeatable mixture of blackberry with apple, is a firm favourite in my family, and my friends love it, too. I make it in large quantities every year and we never have enough! Not only is it a wonderful spreading jam, but I use it in tarts and cakes as well.

700 g (1½ lb) cooking apples (tart green apples), peeled, cored and chopped
1.1 kg (2½ lb) blackberries, hulled
1.4 kg (3 lb/6 cups) sugar

Put the apples and blackberries into a preserving pan with a small amount of water. Bring gently to simmering point and simmer for 6–8 minutes until the fruit has softened.

Add the sugar and stir until dissolved. Bring to the boil and boil rapidly until setting point is reached.

Pot the jam in warm, clean jars and cover. Seal when cold.
Makes 2.3 kg (5 lb)

Spiced Blackberries in Vodka

Blackberries are almost always so plentiful in early autumn that you can use them for making many other preserves besides the usual delicious jams, jellies and pies. Pickled in spiced vinegar, and with an extra kick of vodka, these blackberries are wonderful with cheese and French bread, or with a plate of winter salad.

450 g (1 lb/2 cups) sugar
300 ml (½ pint/1¼ cups) vinegar
5 ml (1 tsp) allspice berries
5 ml (1 tsp) cloves
900 g (2 lb) blackberries, hulled
5 ml (1 tsp) ground ginger
150 ml (¼ pint/⅔ cup) vodka

Put the sugar in an aluminium preserving pan with the vinegar. Stir over a gentle heat until the sugar has dissolved.

Tie the spices in a muslin (cheesecloth) bag and add to the pan. Simmer for several minutes. Add the blackberries and ginger and poach gently for 10–15 minutes. Remove the bag of spices.

Lift out the blackberries with a slotted spoon and pack into warm, clean jars. Boil the vinegar rapidly until it turns syrupy. Pour the vinegar over the blackberries and top up with the vodka. Cover and seal.
Makes 1.4 kg (3 lb)

Mythology has it that the Crown of Thorns was made from bramble, the thorny twig of the blackberry plant.

Blackberry Cheese

As the blackberry season flourishes, great banks of bramble in a meadow near my cottage hang heavy with ripe fruit. I cannot resist gathering them, partly because I love blackberrying expeditions. Over the years I have therefore had to dream up all kinds of different ways of preserving my harvest. This cheese makes delightful eating all through the winter and well into the following spring.

900 g (2 lb) blackberries
300 ml (½ pint/1¼ cups) water
sugar

Put the blackberries into a preserving pan with the water. Cover and simmer for about 15–20 minutes until very soft. Rub the blackberries through a sieve. Return the pulp to the pan and continue cooking for 15–20 minutes to reduce the liquid content.

Measure the pulp into the cleaned preserving pan. To every 600 ml (1 pint/2½ cups) pulp, add 450 g (1 lb/2 cups) sugar. Stir over a gentle heat until the sugar has dissolved. Simmer gently for 10–15 minutes until the mixture is thick.

Grease warm, clean jars with a little glycerine. Pot the cheese in the jars. Cover and seal.
Makes 1.4 kg (3 lb)

Damson and Blackberry Jam

A classic mixture, these two fruits make a superlative autumn jam. The preparation for it takes me to two of my favourite places on an afternoon's walk – a peaceful meadow and a deserted garden – gathering the fruits in the quiet of the countryside. Shiny, dark blackberries glisten next to the pale, dusky-mauve damsons in my basket. Migratory birds are gathering, chattering and twittering; a harvest moon rises in the sky late in the afternoon.

900 g (2 lb) blackberries, hulled
900 g (2 lb) damsons, halved and stoned
300 ml (½ pint/1¼ cups) water
1.4 kg (3 lb/6 cups) sugar

Put the blackberries and damsons into a preserving pan with the water. Simmer for about 10 minutes until tender. Add the sugar and stir until dissolved. Bring to the boil and boil until setting point is reached.

Pot the jam in warm, clean jars and cover. Seal when cold.
Makes 2.3 kg (5 lb)

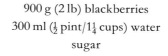

The damson, or 'plum of Damascus', was first brought to Europe by the Crusaders, who found damsons growing in Damascus.

Wild Plum and Date Chutney

A treat for Christmas, this chutney has a festive feel. I like to pot it in special jars, with pretty labels, to give as gifts.

1.4 kg (3 lb) wild plums (bullaces or damsons), halved and stoned
350 g (12 oz/2 cups) fresh dates, stoned and chopped
3 small onions, skinned and finely sliced
600 ml (1 pint/2½ cups) malt vinegar
700 g (1½ lb/3 cups) sugar
15 ml (1 tbsp) salt
5 ml (1 tsp) ground ginger
2.5 ml (½ tsp) ground black pepper
5 ml (1 tsp) grated nutmeg

Put the bullaces or damsons into an aluminium preserving pan with the dates, onions and vinegar. Simmer for 15–20 minutes until soft.

Stir in the sugar, salt and spices. Simmer until the mixture thickens, stirring frequently to prevent sticking. Cool, then pack the chutney into clean jars. Cover and seal.

Makes 2.7 kg (6 lb)

Wild Plum Butter

This crunchy plum butter makes a fantastic sandwich-filler and is also delicious with crème fraîche or cream cheese as a winter dessert.

whole skinned almonds
wild plums (bullaces or damsons), halved and stoned
sugar
ground allspice, to taste

Chop 25 g (1 oz/¼ cup) almonds per 450 g (1 lb) plums. Put the plums into a preserving pan with a little water. Simmer for 10–15 minutes until soft, stirring occasionally. Press the plums through a coarse sieve.

Measure the fruit pulp into the cleaned preserving pan. To every 450 g (1 lb) pulp, add 350 g (12 oz/1½ cups) sugar. Stir over a gentle heat until the sugar has dissolved. Add the allspice to taste and the almonds. Simmer gently for 5–10 minutes until the mixture is a smooth, buttery consistency.

Pot the butter in warm, clean jars and cover with airtight tops. Immerse the jars in a pan of hot water and boil for 5 minutes. Remove the jars from the water and cool.

Autumn Chutney

Gathering the produce of the season as the days shorten, as the sun travels lower in the sky and the earth quietens, is a deeply satisfying pastime. Making the most of the produce is a pleasure, too, and this chutney brings several of the fruits of the season together in a mouthwatering way.

450 g (1 lb) plums or bullaces, halved and stoned
450 g (1 lb) apples, peeled and cored
450 g (1 lb) tomatoes, chopped
450 g (1 lb) onions, skinned and sliced
2 large garlic cloves, skinned and chopped
450 g (1 lb/3 cups) sultanas (golden raisins)
600 ml (1 pint/2½ cups) vinegar
1.25 ml (¼ tsp) mace
1.25 ml (¼ tsp) ground mixed spice
15 g (½ oz/2 tbsp) ground ginger
450 g (1 lb/2 cups) demerara (light brown) sugar

Mix the fruit and vegetables together. Put into an aluminium preserving pan with all the remaining ingredients, except the sugar. Simmer for about 30 minutes until tender.

Add the sugar and stir until dissolved. Simmer gently, stirring frequently, until thick.

Cool, then pack the chutney into clean jars. Cover and seal.
Makes 3.2 kg (7 lb)

Plum and Hazelnut (Filbert) Jam

In a year when my neighbour's plum tree is laden with fruit, I use some of them to make this delectable jam. There is a wild damson in a deserted garden nearby, and I have made this recipe using them as an alternative. Both jams are amazing. Fresh, nutty, with a lovely texture, they are irresistible on newly baked bread, especially the Plaited Cob on page 67.

1.4 kg (3 lb) plums, stoned
1 orange, finely chopped
1 lemon, finely chopped
1.4 kg (3 lb/6 cups) sugar
450 g (1 lb/3 cups) raisins
150 ml (¼ pint/⅔ cup) water
225 g (8 oz/2 cups) hazelnuts (filberts), chopped

Cut the plum flesh into small dice. Mix the plums and citrus fruits in a preserving pan. Add the sugar, raisins and water. Simmer gently for 1½ hours. Add the nuts and cook for a further 15 minutes.

Pot the jam in warm, clean jars and cover. Seal when cold.
Makes 2.3 kg (5 lb)

Apple, Pear and Plum Jam

A rich, fruity jam to make in a plentiful year when orchards and garden fruit trees are laden. My personal combination, dictated by what grows in my garden and nearby, is of Bramley apples, Williams pears and Victoria plums.

equal quantities of apples, pears and plums
sugar
grated lemon rind
fresh root ginger

Peel and core the apples and pears, then finely slice them. Stone and chop the plums. Put the fruit with a little water into a preserving pan. Cook until soft and tender.

Measure the pulp into the cleaned preserving pan. To every 600 ml (1 pint/2½ cups) pulp, add 450 g (1 lb/2 cups) sugar, grated rind of ½ lemon and 10 ml (2 tsp) grated fresh root ginger. Stir over a gentle heat until the sugar has dissolved. Bring to the boil and boil for 10 minutes or until setting point is reached.

Pot the jam in warm, clean jars and then cover and seal.

Greengage Jam

The greengage makes a fleeting appearance every year, never fruiting very prolifically where I live. A friend who has a greengage tree in her garden tells me that it is always a race between her and the birds! If there are any greengages to spare, I make this jam to enjoy at breakfast later in the winter. It is delicious on warm croissants.

1.8 kg (4 lb) greengages, stoned and roughly chopped
450 ml (¾ pint/2 cups) water
1.4 kg (3 lb/6 cups) sugar

Put the greengages into a preserving pan with the water. Simmer gently for 15–20 minutes. Add the sugar and stir until dissolved. Bring to the boil and boil rapidly until setting point is reached.

Pot the jam in warm, clean jars and cover. Seal when cold.
Makes 2.7 kg (6 lb)

The greengage has royal parentage, so to speak, in that it came from Italy to France, where Queen Claude, wife of Francis I, took a liking to it. In France the fruit has been known as reine-claude ever since. An Englishman, Sir William Gage, imported the greengage into England in 1724. He lost the labels, however, and could not remember the name, whereupon it became known as 'Gage's plums', thence greengage.

Pickled Green Tomatoes

The recipe for these pickled green tomatoes was given to me years ago by an old lady who had a large garden with a plentiful annual crop of tomatoes. She used up her unripened ones to make this lovely, fresh, crisp pickle, which is superb with a selection of cheeses.

50 g (2 oz) fresh root ginger
600 ml (1 pint/2½ cups) white wine vinegar
100 g (4 oz/½ cup) sugar
6 garlic cloves, skinned and sliced
900 g (2 lb) green tomatoes, sliced into segments

Bruise the ginger by tapping with a meat hammer or rolling pin. Put the vinegar, sugar, garlic and ginger into an aluminium preserving pan. Simmer for about 10 minutes. Pack the tomato segments into warm, clean jars. Pour the hot vinegar mixture over them to cover. Seal.
Makes 1.4 kg (3 lb)

PICKLED GREEN
TOMATOES
(PAGE 26)

The tomato was until quite recently regarded with great suspicion. Early this century it was whispered to be a 'love apple', unmarketable because it might be aphrodisiac. People said that it was chilling on the stomach, and that it caused gout and even cancer. The tomato only really came into its own after World War I, and its use and popularity have been growing steadily ever since.

Tomato Chilli Pickle

This pickle is wonderful served with a meal of various curries – if you wish, reduce the amount of chillies to your taste!

10 large red dried chillies, seeded, soaked and dried
50 g (2 oz) fresh root ginger
10 ml (2 tsp) ground turmeric
30 ml (6 tsp) cumin seeds
oil
300 ml (½ pint/1¼ cups) vegetable oil
10 garlic cloves, skinned and crushed
225 g (8 oz/1 cup) sugar
30 ml (2 tbsp/3 tbsp) salt
300 ml (½ pint/1¼ cups) vinegar
1.8 kg (4 lb) firm red tomatoes, cut into eighths

Grind the chillies, ginger, turmeric, cumin and a little oil together.

Heat the vegetable oil in a pan until quite hot. Stir in the ground mixture of spices and fry for 1–2 minutes. Reduce the heat and add the garlic, sugar, salt and vinegar, stirring. When the sugar has dissolved, add the tomatoes and cook until pulpy. Check the flavour and add more salt if necessary.

Leave to cool, then pack the pickle in clean, airtight jars. Seal.
Makes 2.3 kg (5 lb)

SWEET APPLE CHUTNEY (PAGE 56), PICCALILLI (PAGE 29), TOMATO CHILLI PICKLE (THIS PAGE)

Piccalilli

You can use a wide selection of vegetables of your choice to make this classic spicy pickle.

2.7 kg (6 lb) mixed vegetables, such as beans,
cabbage, cauliflower, cucumber, celery,
marrow (zucchini or squash), onions, shallots,
peppers, green tomatoes
450 g (1 lb/2 cups) sea salt
4.5 litres (8 pints/5 quarts) water
15 ml (1 tbsp) ground turmeric
20 ml (4 tsp) dry mustard powder
20 ml (4 tsp) ground ginger
275 g (10 oz/1¼ cups) sugar
1.7 litres (3 pints/7½ cups) malt vinegar
50 g (2 oz/½ cup) cornflour (cornstarch)

Cut all the vegetables into pieces of a uniform size. Sprinkle with the salt, cover with the water and leave overnight. Drain and rinse.

Blend the spices and sugar with all but 60 ml (4 tbsp/⅓ cup) of the vinegar. Put into an aluminium preserving pan with the vegetables and bring to the boil. Simmer for 10–15 minutes until the vegetables are cooked but still crisp.

Lift the vegetables out with a slotted spoon and put into warm, clean jars. Blend the cornflour (cornstarch) with the remaining vinegar and stir into the hot syrup.

Boil for 2–3 minutes, then pour over the vegetables to cover them. Seal. Store for 4–6 weeks before using.
Makes 2.7 kg (6 lb)

Pumpkin Preserve

Rich both in colour – a golden orange – and in taste, this pumpkin preserve makes a wonderful contribution to a row of autumn preserves on the larder shelf. Offer it up with the Christmas left-overs, for a really festive meal.

1.8 kg (4 lb) pumpkin, peeled and seeded
1.8 kg (4 lb/8 cups) sugar
225 g (8 oz/1 cup) butter
grated rind and juice of 6 lemons

Cut the pumpkin flesh into small cubes and leave for 30 minutes. Drain through a jelly bag to strain off excess water.

Put all the ingredients into a preserving pan and bring slowly to the boil. Simmer gently for 20 minutes or until thick.

Pot the preserve in warm, clean jars and cover. Seal.
Makes 3.6 kg (8 lb)

Pumpkin Marmalade

Try this wonderful autumn marmalade with a basket of warm croissants and brioches – it is fantastic. I love it on wholewheat toast, too.

1.8 kg (4 lb) pumpkin, peeled and seeded
3 oranges, finely sliced
600 ml (1 pint/2½ cups) water
1.8 kg (4 lb/8 cups) sugar

Cut the pumpkin into small cubes. Put the oranges in a bowl and cover with the water. In a separate bowl, toss the pumpkin with the sugar. Leave to stand for 24 hours.

Bring the oranges to the boil in a large preserving pan, then add the pumpkin and sugar. Simmer until tender and setting point is reached.

Pot the marmalade in warm, clean jars and cover. Seal.
Makes 2.7 kg (6 lb)

Pumpkin Chutney

The variety of shapes and colours of the different species of pumpkins and squashes is one of the delights of autumn. Some of them grow to enormous sizes, others have extraordinary shapes and unusual colours. There is no shortage at this time of the year, and they make excellent chutney.

1.4 kg (3 lb) pumpkin or squash, peeled, seeded and cubed

7.5 cm (3 inch) piece of fresh root ginger

12 peppercorns

225 g (8 oz/2 cups) shallots or onions, skinned and chopped

225 g (8 oz/1 cup) demerara (light brown) sugar

1 green or red pepper, seeded and sliced (optional)

225 g (8 oz) cooking apples (tart green apples), peeled, cored and chopped

225 g (8 oz/1⅓ cups) sultanas (golden raisins)

900 ml (1½ pints/3¾ cups) malt vinegar

salt

Put the pumpkin into an aluminium preserving pan, cover with salt and leave overnight.

The next day, drain off the liquid and rinse the pumpkin cubes in cold water.

Tie the ginger and peppercorns in a muslin (cheesecloth) bag. Put with the other ingredients in the preserving pan. Bring to the boil and simmer until the consistency of chutney. Cool, then pack into clean jars and cover. Seal.
Makes 2.3 kg (5 lb)

Ploughing's begun among the gentle hills;
Wide skies where cloudy cities travel white
Canopy little acres; in the blanched serene
Tent of the heaven wheel the untidy rooks,
And settle, gawky, on the browning tracks,
While man and horse pursue their ancient rite.

Vita Sackville-West: 'The Land'

31

Pumpkin Pickle

Hallowe'en looms and huge, incongruously shaped pumpkins appear in the greengrocers, piled up in all their glory. There are numerous fascinating varieties of pumpkin, all with their particular merits. They make a delicious pickle, spiced here with ginger, cinnamon and cloves.

1.8–2.3 kg (4–5 lb) pumpkin, weight when peeled and seeded
1.4 kg (3 lb/6 cups) sugar
1.7 litres (3 pints/7½ cups) vinegar
15 g (½ oz/1 tbsp) celery salt
two 7.5 cm (3 inch) pieces of fresh root ginger
two 7.5 cm (3 inch) cinnamon sticks
15 ml (1 tbsp) white mustard seeds
10 cloves

Cut the pumpkin into small pieces. Put the sugar and vinegar into a pan and boil until syrupy. Pour over the pumpkin and leave overnight.

Next morning, drain off the liquid into an aluminium preserving pan. Add all the spices, bring to the boil and put in the pumpkin pieces. Simmer for 3 hours or until the mixture is thick.

Pack the pickle into warm, clean jars and cover. Seal while still hot. Keep for one month before using.
Makes 2.7 kg (6 lb)

Sweet Pickled Marrow or Squash

Marrow (squash) turns a beautiful translucent pale green when it is treated in this way. It makes a mouth-watering pickle, one of my favourite ways of using the annual glut of marrows. Lovely with hot or cold roast meats, bread and cheese.

3.6 kg (8 lb) marrow (zucchini or squash), prepared weight (see method)
25 g (1 oz) cinnamon sticks
15 g (½ oz/⅛ cup) whole cloves
1.1 litres (2 pints/5 cups) white vinegar
1.4 kg (3 lb/6 cups) sugar

Peel and seed the marrow (zucchini or squash). Cut the flesh into pieces, about 4 × 1 cm (1½ × ½ inch) long, then weigh it. Tie the spices in a muslin (cheesecloth) bag.

Put the vinegar, sugar and spices in an aluminium preserving pan and bring to the boil. Add the marrow to the pan and cook gently, stirring occasionally, until the pieces are translucent but still firm. Drain.

Place the marrow in a bowl or dish to cool. Re-boil the vinegar until it becomes syrupy, adding any fluid from the marrow pieces as it drains off. The fluid should be reduced to about 900 ml (1½ pints/3¾ cups).

Put the marrow into warm, clean jars and pour the boiling vinegar over. Cover and seal.
Makes 4.5 kg (10 lb)

Marrow or Squash and Pineapple Jam

This gleaming pale gold jam, with its touches of green, is one of autumn's star turns. Delectable on fresh bread or hot buttered toast, it also makes a beautiful base for a dessert tart.

2.7 kg (6 lb) marrow (zucchini or squash), prepared weight (see method)
450 g (1 lb) pineapple, prepared weight (see method)
2.7 kg (6 lb/12 cups) sugar

Skin, seed and cut the marrow (zucchini or squash) into small cubes. Cut the skin off the pineapple, remove the central core and cut the flesh into little chunks.

Mix the marrow and pineapple together and make alternate layers of fruit and sugar in a preserving pan. Leave overnight to extract the juice.

Bring to the boil and boil rapidly for about 10 minutes, stirring occasionally, or until setting point is reached.

Pot the jam in warm, clean jars and cover. Seal when cold.
Makes 4.5 kg (10 lb)

Marrow or Squash Chutney

One classic image of the harvest festival is of piles of monumental marrows (squash), sculptural in their beauty. They make memorable chutneys and jams, of which this one is my first choice. Spicy, with a slight curry heat to it, it is wonderful with bread and cheese.

1.8 kg (4 lb) marrow (zucchini or squash), prepared weight (see method)

salt

900 g (2 lb/8 cups) onions, skinned and chopped

5 ml (1 tsp) mustard seeds

5 ml (1 tsp) ground ginger

5 ml (1 tsp) ground turmeric

5 ml (1 tsp) cayenne

1.7 litres (3 pints/7½ cups) white wine vinegar

6 cloves

10 peppercorns

450 g (1 lb/2 cups) soft brown sugar

Peel and seed the marrow (zucchini or squash) then cut into small cubes. Put in a large dish and sprinkle with salt. Leave overnight.

Strain off the liquid and put the marrow cubes into an aluminium preserving pan with the onions and mustard seeds. Mix the ginger, turmeric and cayenne with a little of the vinegar and add to the marrow with the remaining vinegar. Tie the cloves and peppercorns in a muslin (cheesecloth) bag and add to the pan. Bring to the boil, then stir in the sugar. Simmer for about 1 hour. Remove the bag of spices.

Cool, then pack the chutney into clean jars. Cover and seal.

Makes 3.6 kg (8 lb)

Carrot Conserve

Although the recipe looks improbable, this carrot jam is really delicious. It always takes its place on my larder shelf in late summer as the garden crop reaches its peak. Try mixing the jam with whipped cream and toasted, slivered almonds, then piling it into a ring of boudoir biscuits which have been soaked in orange juice.

1 lemon
450 g (1 lb) carrots, peeled
450 g (1 lb/2 cups) sugar
150 ml (¼ pint/⅔ cup) water

Cut the peel from the lemon and slice it into shreds. Squeeze the juice from the lemon.

Cut the carrots into thin julienne strips and put with the lemon peel, juice, sugar and water into a heavy-bottomed pan. Boil until setting point is reached.

Pour into warm, clean jars and cover with waxed discs. Seal when cold.
Makes 1.1 kg (2½ lb)

Green Grape Jelly

Green Grape Jelly is one of the prettiest of all the jellies on the larder shelf – an ethereal pale green with a glint of gold in it. Delicate and subtle in flavour, it makes wonderful use of the 'trimmings' of the late summer grape crop in the greenhouse or garden.

small, green, unripe grapes
sugar

Use the small green, unripe grapes thinned from the bunches off the vine; they are usually about the size of peas. Place them in a pan with water just to cover and simmer about 10 minutes, until soft.

Strain the juice, and add 450 g (1 lb/2 cups) sugar to every 600 ml (1 pint/2½ cups) juice. Boil rapidly until setting point is reached. Pot in clean, warm jars, cover and seal.

Grape Burgundy Jelly

This jelly, made with good red wine, is excellent with casseroled game, or roast turkey.

700 g (1½ lb) ripe black grapes
300 ml (½ pint/1¼ cups) water
sugar
30 ml (2 tbsp/3 tbsp) lemon juice
150 ml (¼ pint/⅔ cup) Burgundy wine
225 ml (8 fl oz/1 cup) pectin

Crush the grapes, about 225 g (8 oz/2 cups) at a time, in a food processor or blender.

Put the grapes into a preserving pan with the water. Cover and simmer for 20 minutes. Strain through a jelly bag for a few hours.

Measure the juice into the cleaned preserving pan. To every 600 ml (1 pint/2½ cups) juice, add 350 g (12 oz/1½ cups) sugar. Stir in the lemon juice and wine. Stir over a gentle heat until the sugar has dissolved. Bring to the boil and simmer for 15 minutes. Remove from the heat and stir in the pectin. Boil until setting point is reached. Skim if necessary. Pour into jars and cover. Seal.
Makes 1.4 kg (3 lb)

Syren of sullen moods and fading hues
Yet haply not incapable of joy
Sweet autumn I thee hail
With welcome all unfeigned
And oft as morning from her lattice peeps
To beckon up the sun I seek with thee
To drink the dewy breath
Of fields left fragrant then

To solitudes where no frequented paths
But what thine own feet makes betray thy home
Stealing obtrusive there
To meditate thine end
By overshadowed ponds in woody nooks
With ramping sallows lined and crowding sedge
Who woo the winds to play
And with them dance for joy

John Clare: 'Autumn'

A great garden designer of the 19th century, J. C. Loudun, recommended carrot foliage as 'an elegant chimney ornament' for winter. He was talking about the subsequently well-known childhood ploy of growing carrot tops in a dish of water. 'Young and delicate leaves unfold themselves, forming a radiated tuft, of a very handsome appearance, and heightened by contrast with the season of the year.'

People with jaded livers taking the waters at Vichy were given raw carrots to eat once a day as part of the cure and cleansing process.

Salted Green Beans

When the vegetable garden yields a glut of green beans in the summer, try this old-fashioned method of preserving.

runner or French (green) beans
sea salt

Top and tail the beans and cut them into 5 cm (2 inch) lengths, leaving any tiny ones whole. Blanch the beans in boiling water for 2 minutes. Drain and cool.

Cover the base of a plastic container with a layer of sea salt. Put a thick layer of beans over the top. Continue making these layers until the container is full. Finish with a layer of salt. Cover with a lid, and put a weight on top.

Keep in a cool place for up to 6 months. The salt will turn to brine. Check the beans from time to time to make sure that they are not spoiling.

Soak the beans in fresh cold water for 1 hour before cooking.

Pickled Red Cabbage

Pickled red cabbage is a classic, a really useful addition to the larder shelf. I love it with a meal of fresh bread and good cheeses.

red cabbage
sea salt
spiced vinegar (see page 148)

Select firm cabbages with a good red colour. Remove the woody part of the core and finely slice the cabbage. Put the cabbage in a large bowl as you work, sprinkling each layer with salt. Leave to stand for 24 hours.

Drain under running cold water, rinsing well. Shake thoroughly to dry the cabbage as much as possible. Pack loosely into large, clean jars. Cover with cold spiced vinegar. Cover and seal.

The pickled cabbage is ready to eat after one week, and is best eaten within 3 months, after which it loses its crispness.

SALTED GREEN BEANS (THIS PAGE)

Chunky Melon Marmalade

The delicacy of flavour in this marmalade is memorable. The lemon and melon combine beautifully, to make a lovely, pale marmalade that is an elegant contribution to any breakfast table.

450 g (1 lb) lemons
450 g (1 lb) melon, skinned and seeded
150 ml (¼ pint/⅔ cup) water
pinch of bicarbonate of soda (baking soda)
1.4 kg (3 lb/6 cups) sugar
225 ml (8 fl oz/1 cup) pectin

Pare the rind from the lemons, then squeeze the juice. Remove the pith and finely slice the rind with a sharp knife, or put it through a mincer. Dice the melon flesh and weigh out 450 g (1 lb).

Put the lemon rind into a preserving pan with the water, lemon juice and bicarbonate of soda (baking soda). Cover and simmer for 10 minutes. Add the melon and simmer for a further 10 minutes until tender and transparent. Add the sugar and stir over a gentle heat until dissolved. Bring to the boil and boil rapidly for 5 minutes. Remove from the heat. Stir in the pectin and boil until setting point is reached.

Cool a little, skim if necessary and stir once again. Pot the marmalade in warm, clean jars and cover. Seal.
Makes 2.3 kg (5 lb)

Melon and Pineapple Jam

'Epicurean' is not too strong an adjective for this wonderful jam. Its colour is lovely – translucent pale green and gold – and its flavour really delicate. So if you succeed in growing a bumper crop of melons, or there is a glut on the market, here is an excellent idea for using them.

900 g (2 lb) honeydew melon,
prepared weight (see method)
700 g (1½ lb) fresh pineapple
juice of 3 lemons
1.4 kg (3 lb/6 cups) sugar

Cut the melon in half, scoop out the seeds and cut the flesh into little cubes. Weigh out 900 g (2 lb). Remove the skin and cut out the central core. Cut the flesh into small chunks.

Put the melon and pineapple into a preserving pan with the lemon juice and their own juices. Simmer for 10–15 minutes until tender.

Add the sugar and stir over a moderate heat until dissolved. Bring to the boil and boil rapidly for about 10 minutes, stirring occasionally, or until setting point is reached.

Pot the jam in warm, clean jars and cover. Seal while still hot.
Makes 2.3 kg (5 lb)

Spiced Green Figs

For me, ripe green figs conjure up Mediterranean countries: mornings with brilliant blue skies and breakfast in the shade, and fresh figs and thick yogurt on the menu. Spicing this succulent fruit is a delicious way of dealing with it. Delectable with roast chicken or a cheese and salad lunch.

1.8 kg (4 lb) ripe green figs
2.3 litres (4 pints/10 cups) water
100 g (4 oz/½ cup) salt
900 g (2 lb/4 cups) sugar
600 ml (1 pint/2½ cups) white vinegar
15 g (½ oz) cinnamon stick
15 g (½ oz/⅛ cup) whole cloves

Put the figs into a bowl. Mix the water with the salt and pour it over the figs. Leave to soak overnight.

Put the sugar and vinegar into a heavy pan. Stir over a gentle heat until the sugar has dissolved. Tie the spices in a muslin (cheesecloth) bag and add to the pan. Bring to the boil and simmer for 5 minutes. Boil the vinegar rapidly for about 5 minutes to reduce. Remove the bag of spices.

Drain, rinse and dry the figs. Place in large, warm, clean jars and pour the boiling vinegar over them. Leave until cold. Cover and seal.
Makes 3.2 kg (7 lb)

Fig Marmalade

Flavoured with ginger and a touch of lemon, this thick marmalade is a firm favourite with my family. It is delicious on nutty wholewheat toast.

450 g (1 lb) dried figs
225 g (8 oz/1 cup) sugar
grated rind and juice of 1 lemon
50 g (2 oz/⅓ cup) preserved stem ginger, chopped
10 ml (2 tsp) ground ginger

Soak the figs overnight in water to just cover. Strain the water into a preserving pan. Chop the figs and add to the soaking water. Simmer for 5–8 minutes until tender.

Add the sugar and stir over a gentle heat until dissolved. Add the remaining ingredients, stirring well. Bring to the boil and boil rapidly for about 10 minutes, stirring occasionally, or until setting point is reached.

Pot in warm, clean jars and cover. Seal.
Makes 900 g (2 lb)

Figs in Wine

I once planted a fig tree in a cottage garden, against a sunny wall where it flourished. It bore fruit amazingly quickly, and we used to love gathering the soft, ripe figs. I made this preserve so that we could eat figs as a dessert through the winter months.

225 g (8 oz/1 cup) sugar
300 ml (½ pint/1¼ cups) water
10 cloves
rind of 1 lemon, pared and thinly sliced
450 ml (¾ pint/2 cups) red or rosé wine
1.1 kg (2 lb) fresh ripe figs

Put the sugar, water and cloves in a pan. Bring to the boil, stirring until the sugar has dissolved, then simmer for 5 minutes. Add the lemon rind and wine. Put the figs into warm, clean jars and pour the wine syrup over them, including the lemon rind and cloves. Cover and seal.
Makes 1.4 kg (3 lb)

OVERLEAF: FIGS
IN WINE (THIS
PAGE)

Spicy Hazelnuts (Filberts)

Hazelnuts (filberts) coated in a crisp sugar and spice mixture make a delectable confection. The baking brings out the full flavour of the nuts.

60 ml (4 tbsp/⅓ cup) olive oil
450 g (1 lb/3 cups) hazelnuts (filberts)
15 ml (1 tbsp) ground cinnamon
15 ml (1 tbsp) ground cloves
caster (superfine) sugar, to taste

Heat the oil in a sauté pan, add the nuts and toss until well coated. Sprinkle in most of the spices and sugar, reserving a little, then toss again. Place the nuts on a large roasting tray.

Bake in the oven at 180°C/350°F/mark 4 for 45 minutes, turning regularly so that they become brown and crisp. Cool, then dry on absorbent kitchen paper. Sprinkle with the rest of the spices and sugar. Stored in airtight jars, they will keep indefinitely.
Makes 450 g (1 lb)

The sun had stooped his westward clouds to win
Like weary traveller seeking for an Inn
When from the hazelly wood we glad descried
The ivied gateway by the pasture side
Long had we sought for nutts amid the shade
Where silence fled the rustle that we made
When torn by briars and brushed by sedges rank
We left the wood and on the velvet bank
Of short sward pasture ground we sat us down
To shell our nutts before we reached the town
The near hand stubble field with mellow glower
Showed the dimmed blaze of poppys still in flower
And sweet the molehills smelt we sat upon
And now the thymes in bloom but where is pleasure gone

John Clare: 'Nutting'

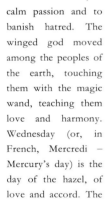

Hazel is an emblem of peace. The ancient Greeks thought that it had the power to reconcile hearts divided by envy and hatred. They believed that Apollo gave Mercury a hazel rod which had the power to impart the love of virtue, to calm passion and to banish hatred. The winged god moved among the peoples of the earth, touching them with the magic wand, teaching them love and harmony. Wednesday (or, in French, Mercredi – Mercury's day) is the day of the hazel, of love and accord. The month of wisdom, August 6 – September 2, is the month when the hazel comes into nut.

There is an old Hallowe'en custom of placing a row of hazelnuts in the hot embers of the fire. Each nut belongs to one girl, and she says the name of her favourite boy with this rhyme: 'If you love me, pop and fly; If not, lie and die.' If the nut jumps, then the match will be a successful one.

They say that if you plant a walnut tree in an orchard, it will kill neighbouring apple trees. To get a good crop of walnuts, and with a better flavour, you must, according to country lore, beat them off the tree.

Pear and Walnut Jam

This is one of the tastiest and most original jams in the world. Although I do not have a walnut tree in my garden, I always use my crop of pears for this recipe. I have been making this jam for years, and my family and friends love it. It makes a very welcome Christmas gift, too: crunchy, fresh and utterly delectable.

1.4 kg (3 lb) pears, peeled
2 oranges, finely chopped
1.4 kg (3 lb/6 cups) sugar
450 g (1 lb/3 cups) raisins
150 ml ($\frac{1}{4}$ pint/$\frac{2}{3}$ cup) water
175 g (6 oz/1$\frac{1}{2}$ cups) walnuts, chopped

Cut the pears into quarters, then slice them crosswise.

Mix the pears with the oranges, sugar, raisins and water in a preserving pan. Cook gently for 1$\frac{1}{2}$ hours. Add the walnuts and cook for a further 15 minutes.

Cool slightly, then pot the jam in warm clean jars and cover. Seal when cold.
Makes 2.3 kg (5 lb)

Pear and Ginger Jam

This combination of pear and ginger is spectacularly good – you could eat it by the spoonful!

25 g (1 oz) fresh root ginger
900 g (2 lb) pears, peeled, cored and diced
100 g (4 oz/$\frac{2}{3}$ cup) preserved stem ginger, cut into small chunks
900 g (2 lb/4 cups) sugar
300 ml ($\frac{1}{2}$ pint/1$\frac{1}{4}$ cups) water
juice of 2 lemons

Bruise the ginger by tapping with a meat hammer or rolling pin to separate the fibres. Put all the ingredients into a preserving pan. Stir over a gentle heat until the sugar has dissolved. Bring to the boil and boil rapidly for about 10 minutes, stirring occasionally, or until setting point is reached. Remove the piece of ginger.

Lift out the fruit with a slotted spoon and place in warm, clean jars. Boil the syrup rapidly for a few minutes to reduce, then pour it over the fruit to cover. Leave to cool. Cover and seal when cold.
Makes 1.4 kg (3 lb)

Pear and Rosemary Jelly

A clear, soft greenish-buff coloured jelly, this is an excellent combination of fruit and herb. My rosemary bush happens to grow underneath my pear tree, and it is still flourishing and full of its aromatic flavour when the pears ripen. The jelly is delicious on toast or croissants at breakfast, and delectable on fresh scones (biscuits).

900 g (2 lb) pears, roughly chopped
pared rind and juice of 2 lemons
medium bunch of rosemary
sugar
225 ml (8 fl oz/1 cup) pectin

Put the pears, rind and juice, and bunch of rosemary into a preserving pan. Add enough water to just cover the fruit. Cover and simmer for 25–30 minutes until the pears are very soft. Strain through a jelly bag for several hours or overnight.

Measure the juice into the cleaned preserving pan. To every 600 ml/(1 pint/2½ cups) juice, add 450 g (1 lb/2 cups) sugar. Stir over a gentle heat until the sugar has dissolved. Bring to the boil and boil rapidly for 10 minutes. Stir in the pectin and boil the jelly until setting point is reached.

Pour the jelly into warm, clean jars and cover. Seal immediately.
Makes 1.4 kg (3 lb)

PEAR AND ROSEMARY JELLY (THIS PAGE), SPICED CRAB APPLES (PAGE 45)

Pears in Brandy Syrup

The only way to eat Williams pears is on the crucial day that they ripen, and I select the most perfect-looking shapes for this delectable preserve. It makes a wonderful dessert in the wintry months ahead.

100 g (4 oz/½ cup) soft (light) brown sugar
300 ml (½ pint/1¼ cups) water
finely pared rind of 1 lemon
two 7.5 cm (3 inch) cinnamon sticks
30 ml (2 tbsp) whole cloves
450 g (1 lb) pears, peeled and sliced
150 ml (¼ pint/⅔ cup) brandy

Put the sugar and water in a pan and boil for about 5 minutes until syrupy. Add the lemon rind and spices, then boil hard for a further 5 minutes. Remove the spices and rind, then add the pears. Bring back to just below boiling point.

Pack the pears into warm, clean jars, using a slotted spoon. Add the brandy, then top up with the syrup. Cool and seal.
Makes 900 g (2 lb)

Pears in Red Wine

Tall storage jars filled with these preserved pears look lovely on the larder shelf – the liquid is pale red, and the pears retain their golden colour in the wine syrup. This makes a wonderful winter dessert for later in the year, served with crème fraîche or thick Greek yogurt.

225 g (8 oz/1 cup) sugar
300 ml (½ pint/1¼ cups) water
7.5 cm (3 inch) cinnamon stick
rind of ½ lemon, pared and thinly sliced
300 ml (½ pint/1¼ cups) red wine
900 g (2 lb) pears, peeled, sliced and quartered

Put the sugar, water and cinnamon into a pan. Bring to the boil, stirring until the sugar has dissolved, then simmer for 5 minutes. Add the lemon rind and stir in the red wine.

Put the pears into large, clean jars and pour the red wine mixture, including the lemon rind and cinnamon, over them. Seal and store in a cool, dark place.
Makes 1.1 kg (2½ lb)

Spiced Crab Apples

In one of the hedgerows where I walk in autumn, there stands a row of crab apple trees, quaint little trees that fruit abundantly in September. One bears green fruit, one or two have rosy apples on them, another has bright, dark red ones. This recipe for spiced crab apples makes a mouthwatering addition to a meal of bread, cheese and pickles.

25 g (1 oz/¼ cup) whole cloves
25 g (1 oz) cinnamon stick
25 g (1 oz/¼ cup) allspice berries
1.4 kg (3 lb/6 cups) demerara (light brown) sugar
1.1 litres (2 pints/5 cups) white vinegar
2.3 kg (5 lb) ripe crab apples, quartered and cored

Tie the spices in a muslin (cheesecloth) bag. Dissolve the sugar in the vinegar in a pan over a gentle heat. Add the spices and boil for 5 minutes.

Remove the bag of spices from the pan. Add the crab apples (do not peel them) and poach very gently for about 5 minutes until tender, being careful not to let them become mushy.

Remove the crab apples from the vinegar with a slotted spoon. Pack into warm, clean jars. Reboil the liquid until it thickens and turns syrupy, then fill the jars to the brim. Seal.
Makes 3.6 kg (8 lb)

Crunchy Harvest Butter

I invented this recipe early one October when the crop of crab apples, by then really ripe, was nearing its end, and I had more windfalls off my apple tree than I could think what to do with. An old-fashioned 'butter' is simply a fruit purée preserved in sugar. Adding nuts to this thick purée, and a little crunchy wheatgerm, gives it a texture which is quite mouthwatering – irresistible on freshly baked bread.

1.4 kg (3 lb) cooking apples (tart green apples) and crab apples, chopped
1 litre (1¾ pints/4¼ cups) water
sugar
100 g (4 oz/1 cup) walnuts, finely chopped
60 ml (4 tbsp/⅓ cup) crunchy natural wheatgerm

Put the apples and crab apples into a preserving pan and cover with the water. Bring to the boil and simmer gently for about 1 hour until really soft and pulpy. Using a wooden spoon, press the apple pulp through a nylon sieve.

Measure the purée into the cleaned pan. To every 600 ml (1 pint/2½ cups) purée, add 350 g (12 oz/1½ cups) sugar. Stir over a gentle heat until the sugar has dissolved. Bring to the boil and boil for 30–45 minutes until the mixture is thick and like jam in consistency. Stir in the walnuts and wheatgerm.

Pot the butter in warm, clean jars and cover with airtight tops. Immerse the jars in a pan of hot water and boil for 5 minutes. Remove the jars from the water and cool. Store in a dark, dry, cool place.
Makes 2.3 kg (5 lb)

In the old days a traditional autumn game for young girls was to pick crab apples from the hedge and lay them out in a hiding place, in the shape of the initials of the boy each girl had her eye on. As dawn broke on old Michaelmas day, October 11th, they would creep out of bed to look at them. The initials in the best condition were those of the husband-to-be of the girl who had put them there.

Medlar Jelly

Known to the ancients, the medlar tree was widely used by country housewives of the past. It grows only in the Old World and is found in central and southern England. I know of only one medlar tree in my part of the world, a pretty little tree that bears odd-looking, quaint brownish fruits each autumn. It has an old-fashioned feel to it and I am very fond of it. To me the medlar, with its distinctive fruit, is one of the most evocative trees of the English countryside – and worth seeking out for visitors to the country. This savoury jelly takes pride of place on a cold table of salads. I use the leftover pulp for Medlar Marmalade (page 49).

1.4 kg (3 lb) ripe medlars, halved
1 lemon, chopped
juice of 2 lemons
sugar

Put the medlars, lemon and lemon juice into a preserving pan. Simmer for about 2 hours or until the juice is drawn out and the fruit is pulpy. Strain through a jelly bag for a few hours.

Measure the juice into the cleaned preserving pan. To every 600 ml (1 pint/2½ cups) juice, add 350 g (12 oz/1½ cups) sugar. Stir over a gentle heat until the sugar has dissolved. Bring to the boil and boil until setting point is reached.

Pour the jelly into warm, clean jars and cover. Seal.

Medlar Marmalade

I make full use of the relatively rare medlar by utilizing the fruit pulp left after making medlar jelly. Essentially this is a fruit 'cheese', but its flavour merits the title 'marmalade'. It is wonderful on wholewheat toast, accompanied by a jug of fresh coffee.

medlar pulp (from making Medlar
Jelly – see page 48)
finely grated rind and juice of 2 oranges
sugar

Rub the fruit pulp left from making Medlar Jelly through a sieve. Add the orange rind and juice.

Measure the fruit pulp into a preserving pan. Stir in 350 g (12 oz/1½ cups) sugar to each 450 g (1 lb) fruit. Boil together until it thickens and setting point is reached.

Pot the marmalade in warm, clean jars and cover. Seal.

Japonica (Japanese Quince) Jelly

Japonica, or Japanese quince, fruits relatively early, before its glossy dark-green leaves fall. Small and unevenly rounded, the pale-golden fruits look unpromising, yet they yield a beautiful and distinctive jelly, which goes well with savoury foods. A welcome addition to the row of jellies that stand on the larder shelf in the winter.

900 g (2 lb) japonica (Japanese quince) fruits,
cut in half
60 ml (4 tbsp/⅓ cup) lemon juice
sugar

Put the japonica (Japanese quince) fruits into a preserving pan with water to cover. Simmer for about 25 minutes until soft. Add the lemon juice. Strain through a jelly bag for several hours or overnight.

Measure the liquid into the cleaned preserving pan. To every 600 ml (1 pint/2½ cups)

juice, add 350 g (12 oz/1½ cups) sugar. Stir over a gentle heat until the sugar has dissolved. Bring to the boil and boil rapidly until setting point is reached.

Cool slightly, then pour the jelly into warm, clean jars and cover. Seal when cold.
Makes 1.4 kg (3 lb)

Cotignac

Thick and with the most beautiful russet colour, this memorable French recipe makes a gourmet dessert served with fromage frais.

2 oranges
700 g (1½ lb) quinces, quartered,
cored and roughly chopped
350 g (12 oz/1½ cups) sugar
100 g (4 oz/⅔ cup) candied peel (optional)

Grate the rind from one of the oranges. Cut the oranges into quarters and put into a preserving pan with the quinces. Add water to cover. Simmer for about 1 hour until the fruit is completely soft. Remove the orange quarters.

Purée the remaining pulp in a blender. Return the purée to the cleaned preserving pan. Add the sugar and the candied peel, if using, and cook until thick, stirring all the time.

Pot the conserve in warm, clean jars and cover. Seal.
Makes 900 g (2 lb)

Sweet rain that changes nature with the soil,
Wet leaves that fade
And lose so soon the weight of summer's shade,
So lightly shedding care,
So soon, curled homes for spiders, spin in air,
Or like pale butterflies adventure flight,
On passers' hats alight,
Play ghosts round children's feet
And stirred again drift careless anywhere

Lucy Boston: ' Autumn Rain'

Ripe medlars – called 'bletted' medlars, which means that they are soft to the touch, dark brown and acidly aromatic – were loved by the dons at ancient universities, who would enjoy them with the colleges' vintage port. In Victorian times medlars were often kept on the sideboard in a silver dish of moist sawdust until they were really ripe.

An old-fashioned family game, when the evenings were drawing in, centred around a basket of medlars. Three coins were pressed into three of the medlars without anyone seeing which ones. The father or mother would then deal out two medlars for each child, putting two aside for a beggar who might come to the door. The parent would tell the youngest to take out two medlars for himself, plus two for the poor man. The basket was handed around to the others in the same way, and when it was empty everyone examined their fruit to find the treasure. If the coins were in the beggar's medlars, the first poor man to turn up the next day was given the money.

Spiced Quinces

I gather a few of the best, firmest quinces for this recipe, which is a perennial favourite. It is always a surprise to me how this hard, golden-coloured, knobbly fruit turns a deep russet red when it is cooked, and has the most amazing flavour. The simple spicing with coriander is wonderful. Spiced quinces take a while to make, but you will be glad you took the trouble!

quinces, peeled and cored
salt
white sugar
white vinegar
coriander seeds

Reserve the peel and seeds of the quinces as you prepare them. Quarter the fruit and cut the quarters into thick slices. Cover with cold water and add 15 ml (1 tbsp) salt to every 1.8 kg (4 lb) of quinces. Bring to the boil and boil for 8 minutes, then strain.

Put the peel and seeds into a pan. Cover generously with cold water and simmer gently for 30 minutes, then strain off into a bowl.

Measure the juice into an aluminium preserving pan. To each 600 ml (1 pint/2½ cups) juice, add 450 g (1 lb/2 cups) sugar, 150 ml (¼ pint/⅔ cup) white vinegar and 15 ml (1 tbsp) coriander seeds. Bring to the boil, add the fruit and simmer until tender but not mushy – the fruit should remain in whole pieces and firm. Pour into a bowl and leave until the next day.

Drain off the syrup, bring to the boil and again pour over the fruit. Leave until the next day.

Repeat as before, reducing the syrup until quite thick. Pack the fruit into warm, clean jars and pour the hot vinegar over. Cover and seal.

SPICED QUINCES
(THIS PAGE)

Quince and Cherry Jam

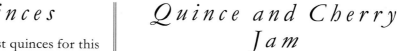

A deep orange-red, this wonderful jam has a thick, slightly grainy texture, which is punctuated by glacé (candied) cherries and almonds. You can use it as the base of a tart, as the filling for a cake, with cream cheese or as an accompaniment to hot croissants and brioches.

2.7 kg (6 lb) quinces, peeled, cored and quartered
300 ml (½ pint/1¼ cups) water
1.8 kg (4 lb/8 cups) sugar
100 g (4 oz/¾ cup) whole almonds, unskinned
100 g (4 oz/½ cup) glacé (candied) cherries
450 g (1 lb/3 cups) sultanas (golden raisins)
100 g (4 oz) fresh root ginger

Grate the quinces on the coarse side of a grater. Place in a preserving pan with the water and simmer for about 15 minutes until tender. Bruise the ginger by tapping with a meat hammer or rolling pin to separate the fibres. Tie in a muslin (cheesecloth) bag. Add the remaining ingredients and simmer gently until setting point is reached. Remove the root ginger.

Pot the jam in warm, clean jars and cover. Seal when cold.
Makes 3.6 kg (8 lb)

Fair is the world, now autumn's wearing,
And the sluggard sun lies long abed;
Sweet are the days, now winter's nearing,
And all winds feign that the wind is dead.

Dumb is the hedge where the crabs hang yellow,
Bright as the blossoms of the spring;
Dumb is the close where the pears grow mellow,
And none but the dauntless redbreasts sing.

Fair was the spring, but amidst his greening
Grey were the days of the hidden sun;
Fair was the summer, but overweening,
So soon his o'er-sweet days were done.

William Morris: 'Kelmscott Crab Apples'

Dried Apple Rings

Every year I gather a selection of firm, ripe apples for drying, and this means that we can eat 'fresh' apples right through the winter.

apples

salt

Peel, core and slice apples, then cut the apples crosswise to make rings. During this preparation, put the slices into a bowl of salted water – 25 g (1 oz/2 tbsp) salt per 1 litre (1¾ pints/4¼ cups) water – so they do not discolour.

Lay out the apple rings to dry on a wire rack covered with a layer of clean muslin (cheesecloth). Dry them at an even temperature – 48–65°C (120–150°F) – either in the oven with the door left ajar, or in an airing cupboard (warm cupboard). The time taken will vary according to the water content of the fruit, but you can tell when the apples are dried as they become slightly leathery and crisp around the edges. Cool them thoroughly and pack into paper bags. (Plastic bags could make them sweat and go mouldy.)

French Quince Jelly

Quinces are transformed in flavour as well as colour when cooked. This jelly is an exquisite dark pinkish-red that defies description.

quinces

sugar

7.5 cm (3 inch) cinnamon stick

Peel a few of the best looking quinces, then slice and core them. Cut the rest up roughly and put into a preserving pan. Cover them with water and lay the quince slices on top. Bring to the boil and simmer until the slices are tender. Remove the slices with a slotted spoon. Boil the rest of the fruit hard to reduce it to a pulp. Strain through a jelly bag overnight.

Measure the juice into the cleaned preserving pan. To every 600 ml (1 pint/2½ cups) juice, add 450 g (1 lb/2 cups) sugar. Bring to the boil and add the cinnamon. Boil until setting point is reached. Put the reserved slices of quince into the bottom of warm, clean jars and pour the jelly over the top. Cover. Seal when cold.

The quince, which was presented to Aphrodite by Paris, was the 'golden apple' of the Greeks and Romans – the golden apple of love and fertility. The springtime blossom of the quince has a faint scent of narcissus about it, which is the scent of love.

APPLE AND
LEMON CURD
(THIS PAGE)

Apple and Lemon Curd

Lemon curd was a childhood treat for me – I have memories of its thick, soft texture, its sweetness and that lovely lemon colour. When autumn comes, I make this apple and lemon curd for my family. Lightly spiced and lemony, it is delectable both on bread and toast, and as a dessert tart filling.

1.4 kg (3 lb) cooking apples (tart green apples),
peeled, cored and sliced
300 ml ($\frac{1}{2}$ pint/$1\frac{1}{4}$ cups) water
900 g (2 lb/4 cups) sugar
grated rind and juice of 4 lemons
50 g (2 oz/$\frac{1}{4}$ cup) butter
5 ml (1 tsp) ground ginger
2.5 ml ($\frac{1}{2}$ tsp) grated nutmeg
8 egg yolks, lightly beaten

Put the apples into a preserving pan with the water. Bring to the boil, and simmer until the apples are soft. Press them through a sieve.

Return the apple to the cleaned preserving pan and add the sugar, lemon rind, juice, butter and spices. Stir over a gentle heat until the sugar has dissolved. Bring to the boil. Remove from the heat and stir in the egg yolks. Cook gently until the mixture is hot, but not boiling, and has thickened.

Pot the curd in warm, clean jars and cover. Seal.

Makes 2.3 kg (5 lb)

*Summer ends now; now, barbarous in beauty, the
stooks arise
Around; up above, what wind-walks! what lovely
behaviour
Of silk-sack clouds! has wilder, wilful-wavier
Meal-drift moulded ever and melted across skies?*

Gerard Manley Hopkins: 'Hurrahing in Harvest'

Sweet Apple Chutney

October days shorten, and the Bramley apple tree on the lawn reaches the peak of its crop as all the apples ripen fully. It is time to make this delicious chutney, which has become a permanent standby in my household.

1.8 kg (4 lb) cooking apples (tart green apples), peeled, cored and sliced small
1.4 kg (3 lb) green tomatoes, finely sliced
450 g (1 lb) onions, skinned and finely sliced
50 g (2 oz/⅓ cup) coriander seeds
15 g (½ oz) dried chillies (optional)
22.5 ml (1½ tbsp) salt
25 g (1 oz/¼ cup) ground ginger
450 g (1 lb/2 cups) demerara (light brown) sugar
450 g (1 lb/3 cups) sultanas (golden raisins)
juice of 1 lemon
60 ml (4 tbsp/⅓ cup) golden syrup (light corn syrup)
750 ml (1¼ pints/3 cups) malt vinegar

Put the apples, tomatoes and onions in an aluminium preserving pan. Tie the coriander seeds and chillies, if using, in a muslin (cheesecloth) bag. Add the salt and leave overnight to draw out the juices.

The next day, add the remaining ingredients. Bring to the boil and simmer for 2 hours, stirring from time to time.

Pack the chutney into warm, clean jars and cover. Seal.
Makes 5.4 kg (12 lb)

During the autumn apple harvest one last apple was traditionally left at the end of one of the highest branches on the tree. If it clung to the branch until all the leaves had fallen in the autumn winds, there would be a good crop the following year.

Windfall Marmalade

An ancient Bramley apple tree stands on my lawn, giving welcome shade to my cottage garden in the summer, and a guaranteed crop of the best cooking apples in the autumn. Invariably there are numerous windfalls, so I make use of them in this delectable marmalade, the first of the season.

900 g (2 lb) windfall apples, peeled, cored and chopped
2 grapefruit
4 lemons
2.8 litres (5 pints/3 quarts) water
2.3 kg (5 lb/10 cups) sugar

Prepare the apples, reserving the cores and peel. Pare the rind of the grapefruit and lemons as thinly as possible, using a potato peeler or sharp knife. Finely shred the rind. Remove the pith from the fruits and roughly chop the flesh, removing and reserving any pips.

Tie the citrus pith, pips, apple peel and cores in a muslin (cheesecloth) bag. Put all the fruit into a preserving pan with the shredded rind, water and muslin bag. Bring to the boil, then simmer gently for about 2¼ hours until the peel is soft and the contents of the pan reduced by half.

Remove the muslin bag, squeezing well into the pan. Add the sugar and stir until dissolved. Boil rapidly for 15–20 minutes or until setting point is reached.

Take the pan off the heat and remove any scum with a slotted spoon. Leave to stand for 15 minutes, then stir to distribute the peel. Pot the marmalade in warm, clean jars and cover. Seal immediately.
Makes 4 kg (9 lb)

Season of mists and mellow fruitfulness,
Close bosom-friend of the maturing sun;
Conspiring with him how to load and bless
With fruit the vines that round the thatch-eves run;
To bend with apples the moss'd cottage-trees,
And fill all fruit with ripeness to the core;
To swell the gourd, and plump the hazel shells
With a sweet kernel; to set budding more,
And still more, later flowers for the bees,
Until they think warm days will never cease,
For Summer has o'er-brimm'd their clammy cells.

John Keats: 'To Autumn'

LATE-SUMMER FLOWERS

As late summer draws on into autumn, and thoughts begin to turn towards winter and preparations for Christmas, a harvest of many different plants is there for the gathering. Late summer and autumn hedgerows and gardens provide an abundant harvest not only of foods but of flowers, berries and seedheads. These can be preserved in various ways and will brighten up the house through the winter months. As the long summer evenings dwindle, plant material can be gathered from gardens or along country lanes.

Later, when the house is decorated for Christmas, it makes a refreshing change to see natural arrangements and wreaths, made with late-gathered flowers, seedheads, leaves, cones and grasses.

Drying flowers is a simple process – neither time-consuming nor complicated – and you will reap rich rewards throughout the winter months as the last of the summer flowers give pleasure right through until the following spring.

MATERIALS

When preserving and arranging flowers, foliage, seedheads, gourds, etc., you will need the following materials, available from florists.

Florists' foam: Florists' foam in the form of dry foam blocks is used as a base in flower arrangements. Florists' foam wreath bases, balls and cones are especially useful at Christmas.

Wire: Use florists' wire of the appropriate gauge to support flowers, leaves, cones and seedheads after the natural stem has withered. Stub wires come in various lengths and thicknesses. As a general guide, the thickness should be the minimum needed to support the flower or leaf. Over-thick wire is awkward to use and can damage the material. Reel, or rose, wire is very fine and is used for binding.

Staples: Use long florists' staples, or make your own by bending wire to hairpin shapes.

Mastic: This is green modelling material that does not dry out, used for moulding bases for wreaths and rings.

Florists' tape: This rubber-based tape is used for covering wire stems to give them the natural look.

Moss: Reindeer moss and sphagnum moss are the most commonly used for covering florists' foam before plant material is inserted. Reindeer moss, also known as grey lichen moss, is normally supplied dry and sphagnum moss is usually moist. Moss is available from garden centres and florists.

Silver sand and silica gel: These are used as desiccants for drying roses and certain other plant material.

General: Other useful equipment includes sharp scissors, a sharp knife, secateurs (pruning shears), wire cutters, hair lacquer (hair spray), gold and silver aerosol paint, and ribbon.

Air-drying Flowers and Seedheads

Pick the flowers just before they are fully open: fully open flowers shed their fluffy centres and petals when dried. Daisy-like flowers should have their centres visible, but with the petals cupped round them. With sprays of flowers, pick when two-thirds of the flowers are almost fully open. Harvest flower spikes, such as lavender, when half to two-thirds of the flowers are almost fully open. Choose a dry day, and collect in the morning after the dew has evaporated.

Remove the leaves from the lower part of the stems as soon as possible. Tie the flowers firmly in small bunches of individual species, since different flowers have varying drying times. Air must be able to circulate around the flowers – if the bunch is too firmly packed, the flowers in the centre may not dry completely and may rot, go mouldy or become misshapen. It is a good idea to put a rubber band around each bunch, since the stems shrink during the drying process and can dry out.

The ideal place to hang your drying flowers is in a warm, dry, well-ventilated spare room or attic. The temperature should be at least 10°C/50°F; the quicker the flowers dry, the less colour is lost. The flowers need protection from direct sunlight because it fades them, and they also become over-dry and brittle.

Dried flowers are ready for use or storage when the petals or bracts feel papery and crisp, and you can snap the stems easily. Check that the neck, under the flower head, is fully dry, since it usually dries out last. The time taken to air-dry flowers varies from a few days to a month or more, depending on the thickness and size of flower, the weather, and the drying conditions.

HANGING POSITION

Most flowers are dried hung upside-down, since it prevents the neck bending or drooping. Some flowers, however, dry better standing up. Examples include alchemilla, or lady's mantle, astilbe, goldenrod and ornamental onions. Hang them upside-down for 1–2 days, to counteract the wilting that occurs naturally, then stand them in a tall, empty vase so that they are well supported.

Many seedheads, such as teazel, honesty and bulrushes (cat-tail) can be dried right-way-up from the start. Chinese lanterns look better dried right-way-up; otherwise, the orange calyces stick out at odd angles. Hook the uppermost lanterns over a clothesline or hanger to dry.

HYDRANGEAS

Hydrangea flower bracts should be papery and partly dry naturally, by early autumn. Cut the heads with a good-sized stem and place right-way-up in a vase, with 5 cm (2 inches) of water in the bottom. Leave for a week to ten days; the stems absorb some of the water, preventing the flower head wilting as it dries, and the rest evaporates. The same 'trick' works with lavender, yarrow and heather flowers, as well as foliage, such as hosta and eucalyptus.

Hydrangeas make some of the most sensational early autumn flower arrangements. For a certain effect you can use them singly, or in very small numbers, using carefully selected vases which are tall and slim and suit the dimensions of the flower heads. Or arrange a cluster of hydrangeas in a huge basket, with perhaps a few stems of hogweed (cow parsnip) or some eucalyptus.

GLOBE ARTICHOKES

Globe artichokes also make dramatic dried arrangements, picked either when partly or fully open or when the central purple fluff just becomes visible. These are best dried individually, either hanging upside-down, or right-way-up in a wire rack. Secure some chicken wire over a horizontal frame and slot each flower stem through the mesh. The stems must hang freely, so make sure that the wire is high enough.

Try drying the huge seedheads of giant, annual sunflowers in the same way. Corn on the cob also does very well using this method.

FLOWERS SUITABLE FOR AIR-DRYING
Chive, ornamental onion (Allium)
Cupid's dart (Catananche)
Dock (Rumex)
False goat's beard (Astilbe)
Globe artichoke (Cynara)
Goldenrod (Solidago)
Heather (Calluna, Erica)
Hogweed or cow parsnip (Heracleum)
Hydrangea
Immortelle (Xeranthemum)
Knapweed (Centaurea)
Lady's mantle (Alchemilla)
Lamb's tongue (Stachys)
Lavender (Lavandula)
Lavender cotton (Santolina)
Love-in-a-mist (Nigella)
Knotweed (Polygonum)
Pearl everlasting (Anaphalis)
Sand flower (Ammobium)
Sea lavender (Statice)
Sorrel (Rumex)
Strawflower (Helichrysum)
Sunflower (Helianthus)
Sunray (Helipterum)
Tansy (Tanacetum)
Wild carrot (Daucus)
Winged everlasting (Ammobium)
Yarrow (Achillea)

FOLIAGE AND SEEDHEADS SUITABLE
FOR AIR-DRYING
Artemisia**
Coneflower (Rudbeckia)*
Eucalyptus**
Bamboo (several genera)**
Chinese lanterns (Physalis)
Dock, Sorrel (Rumex)*
Foxglove (Digitalis)*
Flax (Linum)*
Globe thistle (Echinops)*
Honesty (Lunaria)*
Hops (Humulus)*
Hosta**
Knotweed (Polygonum)*

Love-in-a-mist (Nigella)*
Montbretia*, **
Peruvian lily (Alstroemeria)*
Poppy (Papaver)*
Pot marigold (Calendula)*
Scabious (Scabiosa)*
Sea holly (Eryngium)*
Senecio 'Sunshine'**
St. John's wort (Hypericum)*
Teazel (Dipsacus)*
* seedheads
** foliage

Dried Flower Arrangements

The most effective and beautiful arrangements made with dried autumn flowers are almost always the simplest and least fussy ones. Allow the flowers themselves to dictate the shape of the arrangement so that it looks free and natural. Choose a container that suits the height and spread of the flowers that you are arranging, and consider interesting jugs, urns and baskets as well as the vases that you may usually use. Old bottles, too, with just one or two stems in them, can look dramatic and even sculptural – the dried heads of allium make an eye-catching arrangement used like this.

Allow the colours to blend, just as they do in their natural environment, so that the arrangement reflects the soft, mellow feeling of the season. For example, echinops with lavender makes a simple yet lovely arrangement, standing perhaps in a bluish jug. White, cream and silver look beautiful together. Instead of mixing the primary colours in one arrangement, keep them separate. Put yellows, golds and rust colours together; or allow the greens, browns and bronzes to have an arrangement to themselves. The occasional dash of colour can highlight a bunch of dried flowers, but in many cases the colours are so beautifully subtle that they stand on their own to best advantage. Simplicity and naturalness are the keynotes of lovely autumn arrangements.

Sunlight and shadows add interest and charm to dried flower arrangements. Good lighting is important, in order to bring out the muted colours. Dark corners of the house will not do them justice.

CONTAINERS

As containers for dried flower arrangements do not need to be watertight, you can choose from a wide range of different and original ones. Generally speaking, containers with strong patterns and vivid colours are most effective for simple arrangements, whereas plain containers can take more complex and colourful arrangements. Here are some possibilities.

o wicker or rush baskets; garden trugs; hanging baskets

o ceramics of all sizes, shapes, colours and glazes both shiny and matt

o clear or coloured glass, both simple and ornate

o an old copper saucepan, an iron casserole, a pewter goblet, a silver jug, a soup tureen

o a wooden salad bowl; lacquered wood containers from Japan or India

o stone urns or garden vases, terracotta pots, swagged urns; a giant olive-oil jar

o Art Nouveau bowls and vases; an old patterned teapot.

Ornamental Gourds

There are numerous varieties of gourd that you can use for ornamental purposes. These include small, yellow-flowered gourds, which come in various shapes: apple, pear, bottle, turban, and spoon, the latter being ball-shaped with a round neck. Large calabash gourds are white-flowered, and mostly club- or bottle-shaped. Among them are the descriptively named 'Caveman's Club', 'Hercules' Club', 'Powder Horn' and 'Turk's Turban'.

Their colours range from greens and yellow-golds to brilliant oranges and bright reds. Some are striped or variegated, and many have textures

that make you want to handle them, with sharp ribs and knobbly skins. Gourds make eye-catching arrangements and are very easy to prepare.

Gather the gourds when they are fully ripe. The stem of a ripe gourd is dry, and fingernail pressure leaves no mark on the gourd's skin. Small gourds ripen throughout the growing season but large, white-flowered types tend to need a longer, hotter period of growth and are harvested after the first frost. When cutting the gourd, leave several inches of stem, and wipe it clean with a damp cloth. Prick a tiny hole in each end of the gourd, for ventilation, then dry in a cool, dry, well-ventilated spot for a month or more. Either hang them by their stems, or leave them on a perforated plate or a rack. Large gourds can take several months to dry.

Dried gourds feel very light in relation to their size, and the seeds rattle when shaken. Once the gourds are dried, you can coat them with a clear varnish or polyurethane spray; this helps to preserve their bright colours. Varnishing unripe gourds can hasten rotting, a frequent problem with store-bought ornamental gourds.

Ornamental gourds look sensational placed on a patterned plate, singly or in small numbers. They also look lovely piled high in attractive rush or wicker baskets, placed on a table or sideboard.

An Autumn Tea Table

Picture the scene. A scrubbed wooden table, a plaited cob loaf, fresh butter and several jars of home-made jams and jellies. Pretty plates piled high with cookies still warm from the oven, and a moist apple-cake. Pick a few autumn branches with red, yellow, and rust-coloured leaves and put them into a highly coloured jug. In the centre place a ceramic bowl full of shiny gourds, or newly harvested blackberries, or apples and pears, and enjoy the fruits of the season.

CHAPTER TWO

Breads, Pies, Cookies and Cakes

October, the season of change and golden light. Hedgerows and woods are now in full autumn colour. Wild clematis clambers over the turning leaves, among cascades of hawthorn berries. Rosehips, elegant, provocatively scarlet, catch the glinting sun. The oak turns to bronze and ochre, the beech tawny, the horse-chestnut rust-coloured. Maples wear bright crimson, or golden yellow, or all shades in between. Soft browns, orange, copper, creams, illuminate the October land. It is often a month of gales, the wild winds tossing the dying leaves, whirling them as they scatter. Scudding clouds presage autumn gales and heavy rainfall. Birds gather noisily for their seasonal migrations, flocks chattering raucously before take-off.

One remaining stubble-field, soft straw-gold, lies unploughed next to the dark soil of neighbouring land already drilled with winter wheat. The waning sun casts long shadows over the land as it sinks behind the trees. Late afternoon, and a light mist rises off the fields, shrouding the sinking sun as it struggles palely through. In the sighing, dripping copse a wood-pigeon chirrs its cooing song; something disturbs a pheasant as with throaty call it whirrs its wings and, frightened, hops to safety.

In the garden, apples are ripening, dropping the occasional windfall on to the grass below with a dull thud. Pears and plums have yielded the best of their crop, and mulberries will soon be finished. If the first autumn frosts have not yet touched it, the herbaceous border is still bright with the last dahlias, and the careful gardener tends his chrysanthemums with solicitous skill. Virginia creeper has turned deep, bright red; the last nasturtium beams bravely from among limp leaves. Milk-white Japanese anemones stand tall beside clumps of Michaelmas daisies, childlike mauve flowers that spell the dying year.

The damp sweet smell of October pervades the listless days. An old wheelbarrow, full of fallen leaves, stands ready for the bonfire as a low sun slants through the smoke that fills the garden. It is time to be indoors. The damp chill numbs fingers and toes and ears; it is the season to light a fire on the hearth and keep snug as daylight dies; for the evenings are drawing in fast. The season for enjoying home-made cookies and cakes, tasting and savouring the flavours of autumn. The season of fruit pies, the first taste of pumpkin, breads baked with fresh nuts succulent from the tree.

Darkness comes early as a silver harvest moon rises, ghostly, over the lingering twilight.

QUICK POPPY SEED LOAF (PAGE 68), POPPY SEED COOKIES (PAGE 68), NUTTY CARROT LOAF (PAGE 82)

Harvest Wheatsheaf Loaf

One of the central glories of a harvest festival display is a giant loaf shaped like a wheatsheaf, surrounded by autumn leaves, dried flowers and garden produce. These loaves look like works of art – which to some extent they are, but not so much so that you cannot make one yourself. The secret lies in obtaining the mould; if you have a friendly neighbourhood baker he may lend one to you. Failing a wheatsheaf, you can make bread in moulds of any shape or size, and they look very attractive and impressive. The basic bread recipe here is for a 1.1 litre (2 pint/5 cup) loaf tin, so you may need to vary the quantities according to the size of your mould.

15 g (½ oz) fresh yeast or 25 g (1 oz) dried yeast (½ cake compressed yeast or 4 packages active dried yeast)

300 ml (½ pint/1¼ cups) warm water plus 30–45 ml (2–3 tbsp/3–4 tbsp)

450 g (1 lb/4 cups) strong white (hard wheat) flour or 350 g (12 oz/3 cups) strong white and 100 g (4 oz/1 cup) wholewheat flour

10–15 ml (2 heaped tsp) sea salt

beaten egg yolk, to glaze

Grease the mould, and sprinkle the inside lightly with flour.

Put the yeast into a cup with the 30–45 ml (2–3 tbsp/3–4 tbsp) warm water, and leave until frothy.

Sift the flour into a bowl with the salt and make a well in the centre. Pour the yeast into the well and flick the flour over the top. Add the remaining water around the edge and mix thoroughly to a dough, using a wooden spoon.

Knead the dough on a floured surface for several minutes until firm and pliable.

Shape the dough into a large bun, put into a large bowl and sprinkle with flour. Cover with a cloth and leave in a warm place for 1½–2 hours until well risen.

Break down the dough and knead again for 3 minutes.

Press the dough into the mould, cover with a floured cloth and leave to rise in a warm place for 1 hour. Brush with beaten egg yolk.

Bake in the oven at 220°C/425°F/mark 7 for 50 minutes until golden. Cool the loaf on a wire rack.

Makes one loaf

Plaited Cob

Plaiting (braiding) bread dough is nothing like as difficult as it might appear – once you have made a smooth, not too sticky, dough it is really just like making any other kind of plait. This bread, made with granary flour, is irresistible, especially when it is still warm from the oven.

50 g (2 oz) fresh yeast (2 cakes compressed yeast)

600 ml (1 pint/2½ cups) warm water

700 g (1½ lb/6 cups) granary flour (strong brown flour)

225 g (8 oz/2 cups) plain (all-purpose) white flour

20 ml (4 heaped tsp) sea salt

milk, to brush

poppy seeds, to sprinkle

PLAITED COB (THIS PAGE) AND BRAMBLE DROP SCONES (PAGE 97)

Grease and flour a baking sheet. Put the yeast into a teacup with a little of the warm water and leave until frothy.

Mix the flours with the salt in a bowl and make a well in the centre. Pour the yeast into the well. Add the remaining water to the flour around the edge and mix to a smooth dough. Knead the dough well on a floured surface.

Shape the dough into a round with your hands, then cut into 3 equal parts. Roll each one out into a long sausage shape, tapering the ends. Plait the 3 strands. Brush with milk and sprinkle with the poppy seeds. Put on the baking sheet.

Bake in the oven at 220°C/425°F/mark 7 for 30–35 minutes. Cool on a wire rack.

Makes 900 g (2 lb) loaf

Quick Poppy Seed Loaf

This mouthwatering bread is a useful standby when you haven't much time. Made without yeast, it does not require hours of rising and is delicious eaten while still warm from the oven. It also makes lovely nutty-flavoured toast.

450 g (1 lb/4 cups) self-raising (self-rising) flour
5 ml (1 tsp) salt
5 ml (1 tsp) bicarbonate of soda (baking soda)
300 ml (½ pint/1¼ cups) milk, plus 30 ml (2 tbsp/3 tbsp)
30 ml (2 tbsp/3 tbsp) water
poppy seeds, to sprinkle

Grease and flour a baking sheet. Sift the flour, salt and bicarbonate of soda (baking soda) into a large bowl. Using a fork, mix quickly to a soft dough with all the milk and the water. Lightly knead the dough on a floured surface for 1–2 minutes until the dough is light and smooth. Shape the dough into a smooth round with your hands. Put on to the prepared baking sheet and sprinkle with poppy seeds.

Bake in the oven at 220°C/425°F/mark 7 for 30–35 minutes.
Makes 450 g (1 lb) loaf

Sesame Herbed Bread

This soft-textured loaf is made with the dried herbs of the spring and early summer. The lovely, aromatic flavours are a reminder of that time of year. The bread goes very well with a bowl of soup at lunchtime, with good butter and cheeses.

25 g (1 oz) fresh yeast (1 cake compressed yeast)
600 ml (1 pint/2½ cups) warm water
450 g (1 lb/4 cups) wholewheat flour
450 (1 lb/4 cups) strong white (hard wheat) flour
10 ml (2 tsp) sea salt
30 ml (2 tbsp/3 tbsp) dried mixed herbs
milk, to brush
10 ml (2 tsp) sesame seeds, to sprinkle

Grease and flour two 450 g (1 lb) loaf tins. Put the yeast into a cup with a little of the warm water and leave until frothy.

Mix the flours in a large bowl. Add the salt and dried mixed herbs and make a well in the centre. Pour the yeast into the well. Add the remaining water to the flour around the edge, and mix to a dough. Knead the dough on a floured surface for 10 minutes.

Shape the dough into loaves and put into the prepared tins. Leave to rise for 6 hours. Brush the tops of the loaves with milk and sprinkle with sesame seeds.

Bake in the oven at 400°C/200°F/mark 6 for 1 hour. Turn out after 5 minutes, then cool on a wire rack.
Makes two 450 g (1 lb) loaves

Poppy Seed Cookies

Poppies seed themselves everywhere in my garden during the summer. There are all kinds of varieties and sizes and colours, and I allow them freely. Some majestic poppies have huge seedheads which I gather for dried flower arrangements, and I harvest the seed carefully – a few for the garden, the rest for these delicious cookies.

75 g (3 oz/6 tbsp) sunflower margarine, softened
175 g (6 oz/¾ cup) light soft brown sugar
1 egg, beaten
175 g (6 oz/1½ cups) wholewheat flour
2.5 ml (½ tsp) bicarbonate of soda (baking soda)
2.5 ml (½ tsp) ground cinnamon
45 ml (3 tbsp/4 tbsp) poppy seeds

Grease a baking sheet. Cream the margarine with the sugar in a bowl, then beat in the egg. Sift the flour, bicarbonate of soda (baking soda) and cinnamon together, then stir into the mixture. Add the poppy seeds and beat again. Put teaspoons of the mixture on the prepared baking sheet. Press down with the back of a wet fork.

Bake in the oven at 190°C/375°F/mark 5 for 10 minutes until golden brown.
Makes 40

Caraway Crisps

By autumn, my little herb garden is gloriously untidy as some of the herbs go to seed – which I allow them to do so I can use them in dried flower arrangements. I harvest caraway, a great favourite of mine, and these crisp cookies are one of my regular autumn recipes.

75 g (3 oz/¾ cup) self-raising (self-rising) flour
2.5 ml (½ tsp) cayenne
2.5 ml (½ tsp) salt
10 ml (2 tsp) caraway seeds
150 g (5 oz/½ cup plus 2 tbsp) sunflower margarine
50 g (2 oz/½ cup) Cheddar cheese, finely grated

Grease a baking sheet. Mix the flour with the cayenne, salt and caraway seeds. Cream the flour mixture with the margarine in a bowl, then work in the grated cheese. Roll out thinly on a floured surface and cut into rounds with a fluted cutter. Put the rounds on to the prepared baking sheet.

Bake in the oven at 220°C/425°F/mark 7 for 10–15 minutes until golden. Cool on a wire rack. Store in airtight jars.
Makes 24

Tis martinmass from rig to rig
Ploughed fields and meadow lands are blea
In hedge and field each restless twig
Is dancing on the naked tree
Flags in the dykes are bleached and brown
Docks by its sides are dry and dead
All but the ivy bows are brown
Upon each leaning dotterels head

Crimsoned with awes the awthorns bend
Oer meadows dykes and rising floods
The wild geese seek the reedy fen
And dark the storm comes oer the woods
The crowds of lapwings load the air
With buzes of a thousand wings
There flocks of sturnels too repair
When morning oer the valley springs

John Clare: 'Martinmass'

Poppy Seed Honey Pastries

Based on a delicacy of Middle Eastern cuisine, these light, sweet pastries are delicious with a cup of freshly made coffee, and can be served like petits fours after a meal.

175 g (6 oz) puff pastry
40 g (1½ oz/⅓ cup) walnuts
40 g (1½ oz/⅓ cup) hazelnuts (filberts)
50 g (2 oz/⅓ cup) sesame seeds
30 ml (2 tbsp/3 tbsp) poppy seeds
45–60 ml (3–4 tbsp/4–5 tbsp) clear honey
beaten egg white, to glaze

Thinly roll out the pastry on a floured surface to a 20 cm (8 inch) square. Cut it in half.

Grind the nuts and sesame seeds to a fine paste and mix in the poppy seeds. Stir in the honey thoroughly. Spread the mixture on to one half of the pastry sheet, then put the other half over the top. Press down the edges, then slit the top with a sharp knife, making diagonal lines about 2.5 cm (1 inch) apart. Brush with beaten egg white. Put on to a baking sheet.

Bake in the oven at 200°C/400°F/mark 6 for 20 minutes until golden. Cool on a wire rack. Cut into 2.5 cm (1 inch) lengths. Eat warm.
Serves 4

Pumpkin Pie

Spicy, light and velvety-smooth, pumpkin pie is an old favourite. Most Americans would not dream of celebrating Thanksgiving without it. This pie is lovely served with whipped cream into which you have sprinkled a little ground ginger and some chopped walnuts.

sweet crust pastry (see page 92)
For the filling
450 g (1 lb) pumpkin, skinned and seeded
pinch of salt
100 g (4 oz/½ cup) soft brown sugar
2.5 ml (½ tsp) ground cinnamon
2.5 ml (½ tsp) ground ginger
1.25 ml (¼ tsp) grated nutmeg
15 ml (1 tbsp) honey
juice of ½ orange
juice of ½ lemon
2 eggs, beaten
grated rind of 1 orange
grated rind of 1 lemon

Roll out the pastry and use to line a deep 18 cm (7 inch) pie dish.

To make the filling, cut the pumpkin into cubes and cook in a pan with a little water for about 10–15 minutes until tender. Mash.

Mix the salt, sugar, spices, honey and fruit juices together, then add the eggs. Fold in the grated rinds and the mashed pumpkin. Pour the mixture into the pastry case.

Bake in the oven at 190°C/375°F/mark 5 for 45–55 minutes until a skewer inserted into the filling comes out clean. Cool a little before serving.
Serves 8–10

Parkin

Parkin is a kind of ginger cake made with oatmeal, a traditional recipe from the north of England. It was the custom to eat Parkin on Guy Fawkes night, November 5th.

225 g (8 oz/2⅔ cups) medium oatmeal
100 g (4 oz/½ cup) sunflower margarine
5 ml (1 tsp) baking powder
10 ml (2 tsp) ground ginger
100 g (4 oz/⅓ cup) golden (light corn) syrup, warmed

Grease a 20 cm (8 inch) round cake tin. Put the oatmeal into a bowl and rub in the margarine. Add the baking powder and ginger. Mix in the warmed syrup and spread into the tin.

Bake in the oven at 170°C/325°F/mark 3 for 30 minutes. Cool on a wire rack for 5 minutes, then mark into segments with a sharp knife. Lift carefully out of the tin when nearly cold.
Makes 8 pieces

PUMPKIN PIE
(THIS PAGE)

Pumpkin Cake

The abundance of pumpkin during autumn cries out for it to be used freely, and this cake puts it to good use. Light and moist, fruity and spicy, it is wonderful with thick Greek yogurt.

100 g (4 oz/½ cup) sunflower margarine
100 g (4 oz/½ cup) caster (superfine) sugar
30 ml (2 tbsp/3 tbsp) golden (light corn) syrup
2 eggs, beaten
225 g (8 oz/2 cups) self raising (self-rising) flour
5–7.5 ml (1 heaped tsp) ground mixed spice
pinch of salt
100 g (4 oz/⅔ cup) mixed dried fruit
100 g (4 oz/½ cup) cooked, mashed pumpkin

Thoroughly grease a 20 cm (8 inch) cake tin. Cream the margarine with the sugar and syrup in a bowl until soft. Gradually beat in the eggs. Sift the flour with the spice and salt and fold into the creamed mixture. Add the dried fruit and mix well. Gradually mix in the pumpkin to a soft consistency. Put the mixture into the prepared tin.

Bake in the oven at 180°C/350°F/mark 4 for 40–50 minutes until a skewer inserted into the centre comes out clean. Cool on a wire rack.
Serves 6–8

The evening oer the meadow seems to stoop
More distant lessens the diminished spire
Mist in the hollows reaks and curdles up
Like fallen clouds that spread – and things retire
Less seen and less – the shepherd passes near
And little distant most grotesquely shades
As walking without legs – lost to his knees
As through the rawky creeping smoke he wades
Now half way up the arches dissappear
And small the bits of sky that glimmer through
Then trees loose all but tops – while fields remain
As wont – the indistinctness passes bye
The shepherd all his length is seen again
And further on the village meets the eye

John Clare: 'Mist in the Meadows'

Keep a chestnut, begged or stolen, in your pocket as a charm against rheumatism. A tincture of sweet chestnut leaves was used in country medicine to cure chilblains and eczema. Essence of chestnut added to the bath water was used for soothing skin troubles.

Le Turinois

The sight of chestnut vendors roasting their fare over an open fire epitomizes late autumn, with its dark evenings, damp weather and the first freezing-cold toes. Hot from their shells is quite possibly the best way to eat sweet chestnuts. In that case, this classic recipe from northern Italy, where sweet chestnut trees flourish, is the second-best way!

1.2 kg (2¾ lb) sweet chestnuts, unpeeled

150 g (5 oz/½ cup plus 2 tbsp) unsalted butter

150 g (5 oz/½ cup plus 2 tbsp) caster (superfine) sugar

225 g (8 oz/1⅓ cups) bitter chocolate, broken into pieces

30 ml (2 tbsp/3 tbsp) water

10 ml (2 tsp) vanilla essence

To make the chestnut purée, put the chestnuts into a pan, cover with cold water and bring to the boil. Draw them off the heat, and take out the nuts, one at a time. Holding the chestnut with folded absorbent paper, remove both the outer and the inner skin using a sharp knife. Simmer the peeled nuts in fresh water for about 20 minutes until tender. Drain and purée in a food processor, or rub through a fine sieve. This should yield about 900 g (2 lb) purée, the amount required for this recipe.

Grease and line a 450 g (1 lb) loaf tin. Mash the chestnut purée. Cream the butter with the sugar in a bowl and blend thoroughly with the chestnut purée. Melt the chocolate with the water in a double boiler or a bowl over a pan of hot water. Stir into the chestnut mixture and mix thoroughly. Add the vanilla essence. Put the mixture into the prepared tin.

Chill for 24 hours. Turn out the cake and serve sliced, with thick cream.

Serves 8

The diarist John Evelyn, writing in the 17th century, reckoned that the chestnut was underrated by the British: 'But we give that fruit to our Swine in England, which is amongst the delicacies of Princes in other Countries; and being of the larger Nuts, is a lusty, and masculine food for Rustics at all times. The best tables in France and Italy make them a service, eating them with Salt, in Wine, being first roasted on the Chapplet; and doubtless we might propagate their use amongst our common people, at least being a Food so cheap, and so lasting.'

Cob Nut (Filbert) Cookies

Crisp nutty cookies make a delicious snack on autumn afternoons when a low sun slants through the turning leaves, and a chill stillness descends on the lanes. Made with cob nuts (filberts) plucked from the hedgerows, milky-white and succulent, these are something special.

100 g (4 oz/½ cup) sunflower margarine
100 g (4 oz/½ cup) caster (superfine) sugar
1 egg, beaten
15 ml (1 tbsp) milk
2.5 ml (½ tsp) vanilla essence
50 g (2 oz/½ cup) cob nuts (filberts), chopped and toasted
175 g (6 oz/1½ cups) plain (all-purpose) flour
5 ml (1 tsp) baking powder
1.25 ml (¼ tsp) salt

Grease a baking sheet. Cream the margarine with the sugar in a bowl. Beat in the egg, milk and vanilla essence. Stir in the nuts. Sift the flour, baking powder and salt together, then add to the mixture and combine well. Chill.

Roll the dough into a cylinder on a floured surface. Cut into 5 mm (¼ inch) rounds. Place on the prepared baking sheet.

Bake in the oven at 190°C/375°F/mark 5 for 8–10 minutes. Cool on a wire rack.
Makes 12

Cob Nut (Filbert) Crunch

There are many varieties of hazelnut, of which the cob and the filbert are the best-known. The difference between cobs and filberts is that the filbert's husk completely covers the nut and extends beyond it, while in the cob it covers it neatly. The common hazelnut has a husk which is shorter than the shell. In the United States all hazelnuts are now commonly known as filberts. I have to admit that I usually make this recipe in double quantities because it disappears so fast. Crunchy and nutty, it is very more-ish.

100 g (4 oz/½ cup) sunflower margarine
50 g (2 oz/¼ cup) brown sugar
15 ml (1 tbsp) clear honey
225 g (8 oz/2⅔ cups) medium oatmeal
50 g (2 oz/½ cup) cob nuts (filberts), chopped
pinch of salt
5 ml (1 tsp) ground cinnamon
5 ml (1 tsp) ground ginger

Melt the margarine, sugar and honey in a pan over a gentle heat. Add the oatmeal, nuts, salt and spices. Press into a shallow 20 cm (8 inch) square tin.

Bake in the oven at 190°C/375°F/mark 5 for 15–20 minutes until browned. Mark into squares with a knife and cool slightly before removing from the tin.
Makes 8 pieces

Cob Nut (Filbert) Squares

There is a constant demand in my family for a supply of flapjacks (oat squares), so I try to vary the basic recipe from time to time. This is the autumn version, with coarsely ground cob nuts (filberts) which give their inimitable flavour to the soft flapjacks. A nourishing, healthy snack in autumnal weather.

250 g (9 oz/3 cups) small oats
100 g (4 oz/1 cup) cob nuts (filberts), coarsely ground
200 g (7 oz/⅞ cup) sunflower margarine
90 ml (6 tbsp/½ cup) clear honey

Thoroughly grease a 20 cm (8 inch) square baking tin. Mix the oats with the nuts in a bowl. Melt the margarine with the honey in a pan. Mix into the nut and oat mixture. Spread into the tin.

Bake in the oven at 180°C/350°F/mark 4 for 20–25 minutes. Cut into squares while still warm. Lift out of the tin when completely cold.
Makes 16

COB NUT (FILBERT) COOKIES (THIS PAGE), WALNUT COOKIES (PAGE 87), COB NUT (FILBERT) CRUNCH (THIS PAGE)

The cob nut is so-called from its shape, likened to that of a cobble. It was for many centuries called the 'cobill-nut'. The filbert gets its name from St Phillibert, to whom the hazel tree is dedicated. He was an abbot who lived in France in the 7th century, and his feast day is on August 22nd, when the first ripe filberts are to be found.

The autumn morning waked by many a gun
Throws oer the fields her many coloured light
Wood wildly touched close tanned and stubbles dun
A motley paradise for earths delight
Clouds ripple as the darkness breaks to light
And clover fields are hid with silver mist
One shower of cobwebs oer the surface spread
And threads of silk in strange disorder twist
Round every leaf and blossoms bottly head
Hares in the drowning herbage scarcely steal
But on the battered pathway squats abed
And by the cart rut nips her morning meal
Look where we may the scene is strange and new
And every object wears a changing hue

John Clare: 'A Autumn Morning'

Hazelnut (Filbert) Macaroons

Macaroons are usually made with almonds – but substituting ground, browned hazelnuts (filberts) is a revelation. They are quite wonderful. I like to serve them with home-made ice cream for a special dessert course, and they disappear like the melting snow.

100 g (4 oz/1 cup) hazelnuts (filberts)
2 egg whites
75 g (3 oz/6 tbsp) caster (superfine) sugar

Reserve 12 hazelnuts (filberts) for decoration and chop the remainder. Toast the chopped nuts under the grill (broiler), shaking them until browned. Grind them finely.

Whisk the egg whites in a bowl until very stiff. Beat in half of the sugar and beat again until the mixture becomes shiny. Fold in the nuts and the rest of the sugar. Put tablespoons of the mixture on to greased and floured rice paper. Press a whole nut into the centre of each one.

Bake in the oven at 170°C/325°F/mark 3 for 30–40 minutes until set and lightly browned. Cool on a wire rack.
Makes 12

Hazelnut (Filbert) Meringues

Meringues made with chopped nuts are in quite a different league from plain ones. If you use those milky, pure white cobs from the hedgerows, gathered on an autumn stroll, the difference is even more marked. These meringues have ground almonds added too, to give them a texture similar to macaroons. For a delicious filling, fold whipped cream into chestnut purée (see page 77), sweeten to taste, then sandwich the meringues together with the mixture.

100 g (4 oz/1 cup) hazelnuts (filberts),
coarsely ground
50 g (2 oz/½ cup) ground almonds
6 egg whites
350 g (12 oz/2⅔ cups) icing (confectioners') sugar

Grease and line a baking sheet with non-stick baking paper. Mix the hazelnuts (filberts) with the ground almonds. Whisk the egg whites to stiff peaks in a bowl. Add half of the sugar and beat again until the mixture is very stiff and shiny. Fold in the remaining sugar and the nuts. Pipe or spoon the meringue mixture on to the prepared baking sheet.

Bake in the oven at 170°C/325°F/mark 3 for 45 minutes. Leave to stand on a wire rack for 5 minutes, then lift off the baking sheet and cool on the rack.
Makes 20

Red o'er the forest peers the setting sun,
The line of yellow light dies fast away
That crowned the eastern copse: and chill and dun
Falls on the moor the brief November day.

Now the tired hunter winds a parting note,
And Echo bids good-night from every glade:
Yet wait a while, and see the calm leaves float
Each to his rest beneath their parent shade.

John Keble: 'Autumn Leaves'

In Ireland the hazel is the tree of knowledge. St Patrick used a hazel rod to banish all serpents from the island. A hazel rod has special powers. Magicians' wands, batons of authority, pilgrims' walking sticks, sceptres of kings, and dowsers' rods have all in their time been made from hazel.

HAZELNUT
(FILBERT)
MERINGUES
(THIS PAGE)

Toasted Hazelnut (Filbert) Cookies

The taste of hazelnuts (filberts) is transformed by the process of browning them lightly under the grill (broiler), shaking them so that they change colour evenly. That special flavour is at its best in these delectably light, crisp cookies.

175 g (6 oz/¾ cup) sunflower margarine
100 g (4 oz/scant 1 cup) icing (confectioners') sugar
100 g (4 oz/1 cup) hazelnuts (filberts), ground and browned
225 g (8 oz/2 cups) plain (all-purpose) flour
pinch of salt
2.5 ml (½ tsp) vanilla essence

Thoroughly grease a baking sheet. Cream the margarine with the sugar in a bowl. Mix in the nuts and beat thoroughly. Stir in the flour and salt and beat again. Add the vanilla. Mix to a dough and knead lightly on a floured surface. Chill for 30 minutes.

Roll the dough into a cylinder and cut into rounds, about 5 mm (¼ inch) thick. Put the rounds on the prepared baking sheet.

Bake in the oven at 180°C/350°F/mark 4 for 15–20 minutes until lightly browned. Dust with a little icing (confectioners') sugar. Cool on a wire rack.
Makes 10–12

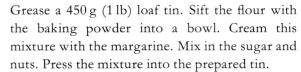

Nutty Shortbread

These tasty morsels are a regular teatime feature during the weeks when fresh nuts are available. As the afternoons become noticeably shorter, and the air chilly with the first mists of the season, nutty shortbread makes its welcome appearance.

175 g (6 oz/1½ cups) plain (all-purpose) flour
2.5 ml (½ tsp) baking powder
100 g (4 oz/½ cup) sunflower margarine
75 g (3 oz/6 tbsp) light brown sugar
100 g (4 oz/1 cup) walnuts or hazelnuts (filberts), finely chopped

Grease a 450 g (1 lb) loaf tin. Sift the flour with the baking powder into a bowl. Cream this mixture with the margarine. Mix in the sugar and nuts. Press the mixture into the prepared tin.

Bake in the oven at 170°C/325°F/mark 3 for 40 minutes until golden. Cool on a wire rack for 5 minutes, then mark into strips with a sharp knife. Leave until cold before turning out of the tin.
Makes 8

Nutty Carrot Loaf

This wonderful loaf is a memorable treat for an autumnal teatime. I remember first tasting it after walking my dog through the fields one September afternoon, watching a low sun light the yellowing leaves of horse chestnuts in the lane. The light, soft texture and amazing taste of this carrot loaf were just right to warm me up.

100 g (4 oz/½ cup) sunflower margarine
175 g (6 oz/¾ cup) caster (superfine) sugar
3 eggs
225 g (8 oz/2 cups) self raising (self-rising) flour
2.5 ml (½ tsp) grated nutmeg
5 ml (1 tsp) ground ginger
5 ml (1 tsp) bicarbonate of soda (baking soda)
2.5 ml (½ tsp) salt
225 g (8 oz/2 cups) carrots, finely grated
75 g (3 oz/¾ cup) walnuts, chopped
90 ml (6 tbsp/⅓ cup) milk

Thoroughly grease a 900 g (2 lb) loaf tin. Cream the margarine with the sugar in a bowl, then gradually beat in the eggs. Sift the flour with the spices, bicarbonate of soda (baking soda) and salt. Beat the grated carrot alternately with the flour mixture into the creamed mixture. Fold in the nuts and milk. Put the mixture into the prepared tin.

Bake in the oven at 180°C/350°F/mark 4 for 45 minutes. Leave to cool in the tin on a wire rack for 10 minutes before turning out. Serve lightly buttered.
Makes 900 g (2 lb) loaf

A forked hazel rod is a water-diviner, but to be effective it must be cut in a certain way: after sunset and before sunrise, and only on certain nights such as Good Friday, St John's day, Epiphany and Shrove Tuesday, and by the seventh son of a seventh son.

Small hazel twigs will protect the house from lightning. Carry a double hazelnut in your pocket and you will never suffer from toothache.

Nutty Carrot Cake

This recipe turns out almost more like a soufflé than a cake – it is very light, yet moist, nutty and chewy at the same time.

4 eggs, separated
225 g (8 oz/1 cup) caster (superfine) sugar
grated rind of 1 lemon
100 g (4 oz/1 cup) cob nuts (filberts), coarsely ground
100 g (4 oz/1 cup) walnuts, coarsely ground
225 g (8 oz/2 cups) carrots, finely grated
15–20 ml (1 heaped tbsp) self-raising
(self-rising) flour

Grease and line a 900 g (2 lb) loaf tin. Beat the egg yolks with the sugar in a bowl until thick, pale and creamy. Beat in the lemon rind. Mix in the nuts thoroughly, then fold in the carrot. Beat in the flour. Finally, very stiffly whisk the egg whites and fold into the nut mixture. Pour the mixture into the prepared tin.

Bake in the oven at 180°C/350°F/mark 4 for 35 minutes. Leave to cool in the tin, then turn out and leave until cold.
Serves 6

Spicy Nut Crackers

These crisp golden crackers have the warming taste of India – the ground spices of 'garam masala'. The juicy nuttiness of freshly gathered hazelnuts (filberts) makes them truly autumnal.

100 g (4 oz/½ cup) sunflower margarine
2 egg yolks, lightly beaten
100 g (4 oz/1 cup) plain (all-purpose) flour
15 ml (1 tbsp) garam masala
2.5 ml (½ tsp) baking powder
salt
50 g (2 oz/½ cup) hazelnuts (filberts), coarsely ground

Grease a baking sheet. Cream the margarine in a bowl, then beat in the egg yolks. Sift the flour, garam masala, baking powder and salt together, then stir into the egg mixture. Mix in the nuts. Knead to a pliable dough. Roll teaspoons of the mixture into small flat rounds with your hands. Put the rounds on to the prepared baking sheet. Press them down with the back of a fork.

Bake in the oven at 180°C/350°F/mark 4 for about 20 minutes until crisp and golden.
Makes 24

At one time the carrot was regarded as an exotic vegetable. Ladies at the court of the Stuart kings pinned the feathery plumes of young carrots into their wide, sweeping hats instead of, or as well as, feathers.

The walnut tree was not introduced into Britain until the 15th century, and the Pilgrim Fathers took it with them to the New World. The United States is the world's leading producer of walnuts.

Nusstorte

Simplicity itself to make, this Austrian recipe makes a light, moist cake. Slender in form, it is amazingly full in flavour – especially if you use freshly ripened walnuts. It is equally good with a cup of tea or coffee, or as a dessert with clotted cream or thick yogurt on top.

25 g (1 oz/½ cup) fine soft breadcrumbs
a little fruit juice
3 eggs, separated
75 g (3 oz/6 tbsp) caster (superfine) sugar
75 g (3 oz/¾ cup) ground walnuts

Thoroughly grease and flour a loose-bottomed 20 cm (8 inch) cake tin. Soak the breadcrumbs in the fruit juice for a few minutes. Whisk the egg yolks with the sugar in a bowl until thick and creamy. Beat the whites until stiff and fold them into the egg yolk mixture alternately with the breadcrumbs and ground nuts. Put the mixture into the prepared tin.

Bake in the oven at 180°C/350°F/mark 4 for 40 minutes. Cool on a wire rack. Remove the base when cold.
Serves 4–6

Walnut Wafers

These light walnut wafers make a delicious savoury snack to go with a drink before a meal.

50 g (2 oz/½ cup) self raising (self-rising) flour
2.5 ml (½ tsp) salt
100 g (4 oz/½ cup) sunflower margarine
175 g (6 oz/1½ cups) walnuts, coarsely ground

Thoroughly grease a baking tin. Mix the flour and salt with the margarine in a bowl, then cream them together well. Mix in the ground nuts. Roll into small balls and flatten down. Put them on to the prepared baking tin.

Bake in the oven at 200°C/400°F/mark 6 for 10–15 minutes.
Makes 16

Cheese Nutters

These cheesey little morsels have the delectable crunch and flavour of fresh walnuts. An irresistible nibble with a drink before supper.

50 g (2 oz/½ cup) hard cheese, grated
75 g (3 oz/6 tbsp) sunflower margarine
50 g (2 oz/½ cup) walnuts, chopped small
75 g (3 oz/¾ cup) self-raising (self-rising) flour
ground black pepper

Grease a baking sheet. Cream the cheese with the margarine in a bowl, then mix in the walnuts. Beat in the flour and season with plenty of black pepper.

Knead to a dough. Put teaspoons of the mixture on to the prepared baking sheet. Press down with the back of a fork.

Bake in the oven at 220°C/425°F/mark 7 for 10–12 minutes until golden. Cool on a wire rack. Makes 15

Walnut Cookies

Kicking through fallen leaves on an autumn walk near the house where I lived as a child, I remember the excitement of stumbling upon fallen walnuts: we scurried for them like squirrels. Among the bright reds, oranges and russet colours of the leaves were hidden these damp, dark brown shells, some with a withering green husk still clinging to them.

40 g (1½ oz/3 tbsp) sunflower margarine
75 g (3 oz/6 tbsp) caster (superfine) sugar
100 g (4 oz/1 cup) plain (all-purpose) flour
50 g (2 oz/½ cup) walnuts, finely chopped
15 ml (1 tbsp) milk
a few drops of vanilla flavouring
45 ml (3 tbsp/4 tbsp) rolled oats

Grease a baking sheet. Cream the margarine with the sugar in a bowl. Add the flour and blend well. Mix in the nuts, milk and vanilla flavouring. Knead to a smooth paste.

Roll out to 5 mm (¼ inch) thick and cut into rounds with a small glass or cutter. Sprinkle with the oats and press down with a fork. Put the rounds on to the prepared baking sheet.

Bake in the oven at 180°C/350°F/mark 4 for 10 minutes until golden.
Makes 12–15

Classic Walnut Cake

This recipe is based on an exceptional walnut cake that we used to buy during my childhood. Memories of it are still vivid: the dry, fine texture of the cake . . . the distinctive flavour of the delicately chopped walnuts . . . and Earl Grey tea. This is my own version of that cake, which lives up to the memory.

200 g (7 oz/1¾ cups) plain (all-purpose) flour
5 ml (1 tsp) baking powder
200 g (7 oz/⅞ cup) unsalted butter
200 g (7 oz/⅞ cup) caster (superfine) sugar
3 eggs
50 g (2 oz/½ cup) walnuts, chopped
For the coffee butter icing
75 g (3 oz/6 tbsp) butter or sunflower margarine
100 g (4 oz/scant 1 cup) icing (confectioners') sugar
strong black coffee

Grease a 20 cm (8 inch) loose-based cake tin. Sift the flour with the baking powder. Cream the butter with the sugar in a bowl, then beat in the eggs, one at a time, until the mixture is fluffy. Fold in the flour, then the chopped nuts, and beat thoroughly. Put the mixture into the prepared tin.

Bake in the oven at 170°C/325°F/mark 3 for 30–40 minutes until a knife inserted into the centre comes out clean. Cool on a wire rack for 10 minutes before turning out.

To make the icing, cream the butter with the sugar in a bowl. Add a very little strong black coffee, just enough to bring to an easy spreading consistency. When the cake is completely cold, ice with the coffee butter icing.
Serves 8–10

The crinkled surface of the walnut resembles the brain, and walnut was at one time used in medicine for brain disorders and head injuries. The young shoots were used to make an ointment for treating dandruff and hair loss. Magic powers of healing were attributed to the oils and elixirs made from the leaves, shells and kernels.

Walnut Banana Bread

As the evenings draw in, and late afternoons grow chillier, it is tempting to warm up with a hot drink and a slice of this succulent, mouthwatering bread. Its soft, moist texture is delightfully highlighted by the crunch of walnuts.

100 g (4 oz/½ cup) sunflower margarine
225 g (8 oz/1 cup) caster (superfine) sugar
2 eggs, beaten
3 ripe bananas, mashed
225 g (8 oz/2 cups) plain (all-purpose) flour
5 ml (1 tsp) bicarbonate of soda (baking soda)
5 ml (1 tsp) salt
75 g (3 oz/¾ cup) walnuts, chopped

Thoroughly grease a 20 × 10 cm (8 × 4 inch) loaf tin. Cream the margarine with the sugar in a bowl. Gradually beat in the eggs, add the mashed bananas and mix well. Sift the dry ingredients into the bowl and fold in until well blended. Mix in the nuts. Put the dough into the prepared tin.

Bake in the oven at 180°C/350°F/mark 4 for 1 hour. Cool on a wire rack and turn out while still warm. Serve sliced, with butter.
Serves 6

Walnut and Pineapple Cake

Incorporating fresh walnuts and chopped glacé (candied) pineapple, this delectable cake is moist yet has a good texture. It makes a tempting treat – something to look forward to after an afternoon spent sweeping the leaves off the lawn, and building the first bonfire of the season.

100 g (4 oz/½ cup) sunflower margarine
100 g (4 oz/½ cup) caster (superfine) sugar
3 eggs
175 g (6 oz/1½ cups) plain (all-purpose) flour
a little milk
50 g (2 oz/½ cup) walnuts, chopped
100 g (4 oz/½ cup) glacé (candied) pineapple, diced

Grease and line a 20 cm (8 inch) cake tin. Cream the margarine with the sugar in a bowl, then beat in the eggs. Stir in the flour lightly and beat again, adding a little milk if necessary to obtain a smooth consistency. Stir in the walnuts and pineapple. Put the mixture into the prepared tin.

Bake in the oven at 150°C/300°F/mark 2 for 40 minutes until a sharp knife inserted into the centre comes out clean. Cool on a wire rack.
Serves 6–8

Walnut Bread

A huge walnut tree, one of the stateliest of all trees, stands in a corner of a friend's garden in the village. By October, when its leaves are turning, the nuts are splitting out of their green skins and dropping, damp and dark brown in their shells, to the ground. It is a race to get there before the squirrels – but every nut is worth the trouble. 'Wet' walnuts are one of autumn's most delectable gifts, and they give a fantastic flavour to this bread.

2 eggs
100 g (4 oz/½ cup) dark brown sugar
450 g (1 lb/4 cups) plain (all-purpose) flour
10 ml (2 tsp) baking powder
10 ml (2 tsp) bicarbonate of soda (baking soda)
2.5 ml (½ tsp) salt
300 ml (½ pint/1¼ cups) milk
150 g (5 oz/1¼ cups) walnuts, coarsely ground

Thoroughly grease a 450 g (1 lb) loaf tin. Beat the eggs well in a bowl, add the brown sugar and beat again until thick and creamy. Sift the flour, baking powder, bicarbonate of soda (baking soda) and salt together. Add the flour mixture alternately with the milk to the egg mixture. Stir in the nuts. Put the mixture into the prepared tin.

Bake in the oven at 180°C/350°F/mark 4 for 45–50 minutes until a knife inserted into the centre comes out clean.
Makes 450 g (1 lb) loaf

Malted Fruit and Nut Bread

In a quiet lane where the road divides just outside my village, there grows an ageing damson tree, its branches heavy with beautiful purple fruit the size of marbles. Standing in the long grass beneath it, I gather ripe damsons for this delicious recipe — a kind of malt loaf with a difference. The fruit is a wonderful texture in the gooey, sweet bread. Serve it sliced, with butter.

350 g (12 oz/3 cups) ripe damsons,
stoned and chopped
50 g (2 oz/½ cup) walnuts, chopped
60 ml (4 tbsp/⅓ cup) malt extract
60 ml (4 tbsp/⅓ cup) black treacle (molasses)
50 g (2 oz/¼ cup) sunflower margarine
50 g (2 oz/¼ cup) brown sugar
225 g (8 oz/2 cups) plain (all-purpose) flour
15 ml (1 tbsp) baking powder
1.25 ml (¼ tsp) salt
1 egg, beaten
90 ml (6 tbsp/½ cup) milk

Grease and line a 450 g (1 lb) loaf tin. Mix the damsons with the nuts. Melt the malt extract with the treacle, margarine and sugar in a pan over a gentle heat until well blended. Sift the flour with the baking powder and salt into a bowl, and make a well in the centre. Pour the malt mixture, egg, milk and the fruit and nut mixture into the well. Mix thoroughly with a wooden spoon. Pour the mixture into the prepared tin.

Bake in the oven at 170°C/325°F/mark 3 for 1–1¼ hours until a skewer inserted into the centre comes out clean. Cool on a wire rack.
Makes 450 g (1 lb) loaf

Wild Plum Pie with Walnut Crust

Coarsely ground walnuts give an irresistible texture and flavour to a pastry shell, especially when they are fresh 'wet' ones gathered from the damp long grass under the walnut tree. The sharp and fruity flavour of the wild plums is highlighted by orange and cinnamon.

For the walnut pastry
175 g (6 oz/1½ cups) plain (all-purpose) flour
50 g (2 oz/½ cup) ground walnuts
100 g (4 oz/½ cup) sunflower margarine
50 g (2 oz/¼ cup) caster (superfine) sugar
1 egg, beaten
beaten egg white, to glaze
caster (superfine) sugar, to sprinkle
For the filling
700 g (1½ lb) wild plums (bullaces or damsons),
halved and stoned
100 g (4 oz/½ cup) demerara (light brown) sugar
10 ml (2 tsp) ground cinnamon
grated rind of 1 orange

To make the pastry, sift the flour into a bowl and stir in the walnuts. Make a well in the centre and add the margarine, sugar and egg. Work all the ingredients together with your fingertips and draw together into a ball. Knead the dough. Chill for 30 minutes.

To make the filling, mix the bullaces, sugar, cinnamon and orange rind together. Spoon into a 25 cm (10 inch) pie plate.

Roll out the pastry into a round large enough to cover the top of the pie dish. With the pastry trimmings, attach a rim of pastry to the edges of the dish and moisten with a little cold water. Cover the fruit with the pastry lid and press the edges together with a fork. Brush the pastry with beaten egg white and sprinkle with caster sugar.

Bake in the oven at 190°C/375°F/mark 5 for 25–30 minutes, covering with foil if the pastry starts to brown too deeply. Cool on a wire rack. Serve warm, with clotted cream.
Serves 4–6

Damson Pie

Instead of damsons in this recipe you could use bilberries or blueberries in summer, or plums in autumn. Serve the pie with good ice cream.

sweet crust pastry (see page 92)

milk, to glaze

For the filling

550 g (1¼ lb) wild damsons, halved and stoned

2.5 ml (½ tsp) ground cinnamon

100 g (4 oz/½ cup) soft brown sugar

15 g (½ oz/1 tbsp) unsalted butter

Roll out two-thirds of the pastry and use to line a 20 cm (8 inch) pie dish.

To make the filling, mix the damsons with the cinnamon and sugar and put into the pastry-lined pie dish. Dot with the butter. Roll out the remaining pastry and use to cover the pie. Press the moistened pastry edges together with a fork. Brush with milk to glaze and cut a few slits around the pastry lid.

Bake in the oven at 220°C/425°F/mark 7 for 25–30 minutes until golden. Serve hot or warm. Serves 4–6

Wild Strawberry Flan

This is a really epicurean treat, if you are lucky enough to come across a patch of wild strawberries that are fruiting prolifically. Otherwise, you could use the autumn crop of late strawberries, which are usually smaller in size than the summer ones.

For the sweet crust pastry

75 g (3 oz/6 tbsp) caster (superfine) sugar

150 g (5 oz/½ cup plus 2 tbsp) sunflower margarine or butter, melted

225 g (8 oz/2 cups) plain (all-purpose) flour, sifted

For the filling

350 g (12 oz/2½ cups) wild strawberries, hulled

100 ml (4 fl oz/½ cup) sweet white wine

225 g (8 oz/1 cup) crème fraîche

100 g (4 oz/½ cup) fromage frais

5 ml (1 tsp) finely grated lemon rind

50 g (2 oz/¼ cup) caster (superfine) sugar

To make the pastry, add the sugar to the melted margarine in a pan, and stir over a gentle heat until dissolved. Stir in the flour and work to a smooth dough. Chill. Press into a 25 cm (10 inch) flan tin.

Prick the pastry base with a fork. Line with foil and fill with baking beans. Bake blind in the oven at 170°C/325°F/mark 3 for 10–15 minutes. Remove the beans and foil and leave to cool on a wire rack.

To make the filling, marinate the strawberries in the white wine for 30 minutes. Mash the crème fraîche with the fromage frais in a bowl and stir in the lemon rind and sugar.

Line the baked pastry case with the cream mixture. Lift out the wild strawberries from the wine with a slotted spoon and use to cover the top of the flan. Chill.

Serves 4–6

In one of Grimm's fairy tales the kind and beautiful girl is driven out by her stepmother one cold winter's day, having been told not to return until she finds strawberries in the snow. Cold and miserable, she wanders in despair, until she chances upon the dwarfs' house. There she shares her crust of bread with them and they make friends. As she sweeps the snow aside from their doorway with their broom, there under the snow she finds wild strawberries growing.

Spiced Pear Pie

There is something both festive and autumnal about the spicing of ripe pears. The flavours of nutmeg and cinnamon, along with those of orange and lemon, make a sensational fruit pie. I make this dessert in late September, as the evenings grow shorter and early-morning mists linger around the pear tree at the top of my garden.

sweet crust pastry (see this page, left)

milk and caster (superfine) sugar, to glaze

For the filling

75 g (3 oz/6 tbsp) soft brown sugar

15 ml (1 tbsp) plain (all-purpose) flour

1.25 ml (¼ tsp) grated nutmeg

2.5 ml (½ tsp) ground cinnamon

grated rind of ½ lemon

grated rind and juice of 1 orange

900 g (2 lb) pears, preferably Williams, peeled, cored and sliced

50 g (2 oz/⅓ cup) sultanas (golden raisins)

15 ml (1 tbsp) lemon juice

40 g (1½ oz/3 tbsp) sunflower margarine, melted

Divide the pastry in two. Roll out half the pastry and use to line a 20 cm (8 inch) pie dish.

To make the filling, mix together the sugar, flour, spices, lemon and orange rinds. Arrange the pears in the pie dish, sprinkling each layer with the sultanas (golden raisins), sugar-and-spice mixture, fruit juices and melted margarine.

Roll out the remaining pastry and use to make a lid. Press the moistened pastry edges together with a fork. Make a few slits in the top with a sharp knife to allow steam to escape. Brush lightly with milk and sprinkle with a little sugar.

Bake in the oven at 200°C/400°F/mark 6 for 20 minutes. Reduce the temperature to 190°C/375°F/mark 5 and continue baking for 25 minutes or until golden brown and cooked through. Cool on a wire rack, and serve hot or warm.

Serves 6

Bilberry or Blueberry Crumble

Either bilberries or blueberries can be used for this delectable crumble.

60 ml (4 tbsp/⅓ cup) clear honey
700 g (1½ lb) bilberries (or blueberries)
For the crumble topping
100 g (4 oz/½ cup) sunflower margarine
225 g (8 oz/2 cups) plain (all-purpose) flour
100 g (4 oz/½ cup) soft brown sugar
pinch of bicarbonate of soda (baking soda)

To make the crumble topping, put all the ingredients into a food processor and blend until it resembles fine crumbs, or mix by hand with your fingertips.

Warm the honey and mix well with the bilberries (or blueberries). Put the fruit into a deep 20 cm (8 inch) soufflé dish and cover with the crumble mixture. Smooth down the top with a fork.

Bake in the oven at 180°C/350°F/mark 4 for 25 minutes until lightly browned. Serve hot, warm or cold.
Serves 4–6

Bilberry or Blueberry Muffins

Bilberry or blueberry muffins, butter, thick cream and home-made jam – what could be better!

175 g (6 oz/1½ cups) plain (all-purpose) flour
5 ml (1 tsp) baking powder
1.25 ml (¼ tsp) salt
50 g (2 oz/¼ cup) sunflower margarine
50 g (2 oz/¼ cup) caster (superfine) sugar
1 egg
100 g (4 oz/1 cup) bilberries (or blueberries)
150 ml (¼ pint/⅔ cup) milk

Grease 20 muffin tins. Sift the flour with the baking powder and salt. Cream the margarine with the sugar in a bowl until light and fluffy. Beat in the egg, then gradually beat in the flour alternately with a little milk. Beat thoroughly, then fold in the bilberries or blueberries. Spoon into the prepared muffin tins.

Bake in the oven at 200°C/400°F/mark 6 for 25–30 minutes until the muffins are risen and golden brown.

Cool on a wire rack for 5–10 minutes before lifting out carefully. Eat them while still warm from the oven.

Makes 20

Blueberry Lattice Tart

A special autumn pastry made with hazelnuts (filberts) is a delectable feature of this spectacular tart. The blueberries, enhanced by lemon and a blackcurrant-flavoured liqueur, fill the flan case, and a lattice of nutty pastry is laid decoratively over the top. It is delicious warm or cold, especially if served with good ice cream or thick Greek yogurt.

For the filling
550 g (1¼ lb) blueberries
150 ml (¼ pint/⅔ cup) blackcurrant-flavoured liqueur
grated rind and juice of 1 lemon
90 g (3½ oz/scant ½ cup) caster (superfine) sugar
30 ml (2 tbsp/3 tbsp) cornflour (cornstarch)
100 ml (4 fl oz/½ cup) water
For the hazelnut (filbert) pastry
175 g (6 oz/1½ cups) plain (all-purpose) flour
75 g (3 oz/6 tbsp) unsalted butter or sunflower margarine
75 g (3 oz/¾ cup) hazelnuts (filberts), toasted and chopped
15 g (½ oz/1 tbsp) caster (superfine) sugar
1 (size 6/small) egg yolk

To make the filling, mix the blueberries with the liqueur and lemon rind in a bowl. Cover and leave to stand for at least 4 hours or overnight.

To make the pastry, sift the flour into a bowl and rub in the butter until the mixture resembles fine breadcrumbs. Stir in the nuts and sugar. Bind the dough together with the egg yolk and add just enough iced water to make a soft dough. Wrap and chill for at least 30 minutes.

Drain the blueberries and reserve the liquid. Pour the soaking liquid into a pan and add the sugar and lemon juice. Bring to the boil. Mix the cornflour (cornstarch) with the water, add to the pan and cook, stirring, until the mixture thickens and is smooth.

Thinly roll out three-quarters of the pastry and use to line a 20 cm (8 inch) flan tin. Spoon the blueberries into the pastry case, then pour the sauce over the fruit. Use the pastry trimmings to make a lattice over the top of the flan. Stand the tart on a baking sheet.

Bake in the oven at 180°C/350°F/mark 4 for 45 minutes. Serve warm or cold, with ice cream.
Serves 4–6

Blueberry Cream Cheese Tart

Luscious ripe blueberries with soft cream cheese and sour cream make a wonderful combination. This is an open tart, which is simple to make yet attractive. The flavours are memorably fresh.

sweet crust pastry (see page 92)
For the filling
100 g (4 oz) full fat soft cheese (cream cheese)
50 ml (2 fl oz/¼ cup) sour cream
grated rind of 1 small lemon
5–10 ml (1–2 tsp) sugar, to taste
a little grated nutmeg
700 g (1½ lb) blueberries
50 g (2 oz/¼ cup) caster (superfine) sugar
icing (confectioners') sugar, to dust

Roll out the pastry and use to line a 23 cm (9 inch) tart tin. Chill for 30 minutes. Bake blind (see page 92) for 15 minutes. Cool.

To make the filling, beat the soft (cream) cheese, sour cream and grated lemon rind together, then sweeten with sugar to taste. Add a little grated nutmeg.

Put the blueberries into a pan and heat gently. As they release their juices, add the sugar and cook very gently until the juices turn syrupy. Be careful not to overcook them – they should not go mushy. Remove from the heat.

To assemble, spread the cream mixture evenly over the pastry case and distribute the berries carefully on top. Chill. To serve, dust with sifted icing sugar, then cut into wedges.
Serves 4–6

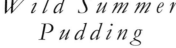

Wild Summer Pudding

Summer pudding is usually made with redcurrants and the summer crop of soft fruits. However, you can equally well use the autumnal harvest of blackberries, mulberries, late raspberries and strawberries – and I pop a few frozen bilberries in for good measure.

8–10 thin slices day-old bread
30–45 ml (2–3 tbsp/3–4 tbsp) water
150 g (5 oz/½ cup plus 2 tbsp) caster (superfine) sugar
900 g (2 lb) mixed berries, such as bilberries, raspberries, blackberries, mulberries, strawberries

Rinse a 700 g (1½ lb) pudding basin (bowl) with cold water. Trim the crusts from the bread. Line the basin with most of the bread, cut into strips or wedges where appropriate. Press firmly against the sides.

Heat the water and sugar together in a pan for a few minutes to make a syrup. Add the fruits and stir together for 2–3 minutes in the hot syrup. Remove from the heat and strain off about 150 ml (¼ pint/⅔ cup) of the fruit juices.

Put the fruit, with the rest of the juices, into the lined basin and place the remaining bread slices on top. Cover with a plate, putting a weight on the plate to press it down. Stand the basin on another plate in the refrigerator and leave for several hours or overnight.

Boil the reserved juices hard until syrupy, then leave until cold – several hours or overnight, preferably. When ready to serve, invert the pudding on to a serving dish and pour the reserved juices over it. Serve with cream or thick yogurt.
Serves 6

Long bramble stems were used by thatchers in the old days to bind the thatch down, because it would protect the house from evil and witches.

Raspberry and Chocolate Gâteau

If ever temptation had an incarnation, this is it: a rich yet light chocolate cake with a filling of autumn raspberries and home-made greengage jam. It makes a good 'celebration' cake but is *not* for waistline-watchers.

100 g (4 oz/⅔ cup) good quality plain (semi-sweet) chocolate, chopped
100 g (4 oz/½ cup) unsalted butter
150 g (5 oz/½ cup plus 2 tbsp) caster (superfine) sugar
3 eggs, separated
50 g (2 oz/½ cup) almond macaroons, chopped
pinch of salt
50 g (2 oz/½ cup) plain (all-purpose) flour
30 ml (2 tbsp/3 tbsp) Greengage Jam (see page 26)
150 ml (¼ pint/⅔ cup) thick Greek yogurt
225 g (8 oz/1⅔ cups) raspberries, hulled
icing (confectioners') sugar, to dust

Grease a 20 cm (8 inch) sandwich tin (layer cake pan). Melt the chocolate in a bowl over a pan of hot water, or in a microwave oven. Cream the butter with 100 g (4 oz/½ cup) of the sugar in a bowl. Beat in the egg yolks until pale. Stir in the chocolate and fold in the almond macaroons.

Whisk the egg whites with the salt until very stiff. Whisk in the remaining sugar until the mixture is stiff and glossy. Fold half of the egg white into the chocolate mixture, followed by the flour. Fold in the remaining egg white very gently. Spoon into the prepared tin and smooth down the surface.

Bake in the oven at 180°C/350°F/mark 4 for 40–45 minutes. Cool in the tin for 10 minutes, then turn out carefully and leave to cool.

No more than 3 hours before you plan to serve it, cut the cake in half horizontally and spread the bottom half with the jam. Spread the yogurt over the top of the jam, then arrange the raspberries on top of the yogurt. Place the other half of the cake on top. Dust with icing (confectioners') sugar. Serve within 3 hours.
Serves 6

Blackberry Crisp

There are few, if any, autumnal treats that I enjoy more than this one. At their peak blackberries have an unbeatable flavour. Combined with a crunchy topping of oats and hazelnuts (filberts), they are epicurean. Thick Greek yogurt goes wonderfully well with this exceptional dessert.

For the filling
900 g (2 lb) blackberries, hulled
100 g (4 oz/½ cup) caster (superfine) sugar
10 ml (2 tsp) ground cinnamon
30 ml (2 tbsp/3 tbsp) lemon juice
For the topping
100 g (4 oz/½ cup) sunflower margarine
150 g (5 oz/½ cup plus 2 tbsp) soft brown sugar
100 g (4 oz/1 cup) plain (all-purpose) flour
225 g (8 oz/2⅔ cups) oats
75 g (3 oz/¾ cup) hazelnuts (filberts), finely chopped

To make the filling, sprinkle the blackberries with the sugar in a bowl and mix well. Set aside for 10 minutes to draw out the juices. Fold in the cinnamon and lemon juice. Put into a shallow ovenproof dish.

To make the topping, melt the margarine in a pan, add the sugar and stir over a low heat until well combined. Stir in the flour, then crumble in the oats. Stir the nuts into the mixture. Put this mixture evenly over the blackberries and press down lightly.

Bake in the oven at 200°C/400°F/mark 6 for 15–20 minutes until the topping is light golden in colour. Eat hot, warm or cold, with cream or thick yogurt.
Serves 6

Bramble Drop Scones

Drop scones (biscuits) with freshly gathered blackberries added to the batter are simply delicious. Quickly and easily made, and eaten hot from the pan, they are especially memorable when served with butter or with clotted (or whipped) cream.

225 g (8 oz/2 cups) plain (all-purpose) flour
2.5 ml (½ tsp) salt
10 ml (2 tsp) cream of tartar
5 ml (1 tsp) bicarbonate of soda (baking soda)
25 g (1 oz/2 tbsp) caster (superfine) sugar
2 eggs
225 ml (8 fl oz/1 cup) milk
15 ml (1 tbsp) golden (light corn) syrup, warmed
175 g (6 oz/1 cup) ripe blackberries

Sift the flour, salt, cream of tartar and bicarbonate of soda (baking soda) together in a bowl, and add the sugar. Beat the eggs and add to the milk and syrup. Make a well in the centre of the flour and pour in the milk mixture with the blackberries. Mix to a batter.

Put 15 ml (1 tbsp) of the mixture on a hot, well-greased frying pan or griddle. Cook until golden on both sides and cooked through. Serve immediately.
Makes 12

How slow the darkness comes, once daylight's gone,
A slowness natural after English day,
So unimpassioned, tardy to move on,
No southern violence that burns away,
Ardent to live, and eager to be done.
The twilight lingers, etching tree on sky;
The gap's a portal on the ridge's crest;
The partridge coveys call beyond the rye;
Still some red bar of sunset cracks the west;
The orange harvest-moon like a dull sun
Rolls silent up the east above the hill;
Earth like a sleeper breathes, and all is still
This hour of after-day, the dying day's bequest,
This autumn dusk, when neither day nor night
Urges a man to strive or sleep; he stands
Filled with the calm of that familiar place,
Idle the shaft beneath his folded hands,
He who must work the lowlands of his farm,
Making tenacity his only creed,
Taking of death and birth his daily need,
Viewing mortality without alarm.

Vita Sackville-West: 'The Land'

If the blackberry comes into flower in early June, then an early harvest can be expected.

Chocolate and Blackberry Brownies

These dark, moist, chocolate squares, light and gooey, contain a surprise when you sink your teeth into them – the delightful fresh juiciness of blackberries. My children and their friends love this way of using blackberries – a plateful disappears in no time.

3 eggs

175 g (6 oz/¾ cup) caster (superfine) sugar

175 g (6 oz/1 cup) plain (semi-sweet) chocolate, broken into pieces

150 g (5 oz/½ cup plus 2 tbsp) sunflower margarine

100 g (4 oz/1 cup) plain (all-purpose) flour

225 g (8 oz/1½ cups) ripe blackberries, hulled

100 g (4 oz/⅔ cup) chocolate chips

Grease a 40 cm (16 inch) square tin. Beat the eggs with the sugar in a bowl. Melt the chocolate and margarine in a bowl over a pan of hot water or in a microwave oven. Mix the egg and chocolate mixtures together. Stir in the flour and beat thoroughly. Mix in the blackberries and chocolate chips. Put the mixture into the prepared tin.

Bake in the oven at 180°C/350°F/mark 4 for 25–30 minutes. Cool on a wire rack and cut into squares. Remove from the tin when completely cold.

Makes 16

The village sleeps in mist from morn till noon
And if the sun wades thro tis wi a face
Beamless and pale and round as if the moon
When done the journey of its nightly race
Had found him sleeping and supplyd his place

John Clare: 'The Shepherd's Calendar'

CHOCOLATE
AND
BLACKBERRY
BROWNIES
(PAGE 98) WITH
BILBERRY OR
BLUEBERRY
CRUMBLE
(PAGE 93)

Blackberry and Apple Crumble

This classic dessert, in spite of being so simple, is one of autumn's great recipes. There is nothing in the world like the combination of blackberry and apple, and to my mind a crumble topping is far better than a pie. The joy of walking through the lanes and fields gathering a basketful of blackberries and picking up windfalls off the wet grass intensifies the pleasure of this lovely dessert.

For the crumble topping
100 g (4 oz/½ cup) sunflower margarine
225 g (8 oz/2 cups) plain (all-purpose) flour
100 g (4 oz/½ cup) soft brown sugar
pinch of bicarbonate of soda (baking soda)
2.5 ml (½ tsp) ground ginger

For the filling
450 g (1 lb/3 cups) blackberries, hulled
225 g (8 oz/2 cups) apples, peeled, cored
and finely sliced
50 g (2 oz/¼ cup) sugar

To make the topping, put the crumble ingredients into a food processor and blend until it resembles fine breadcrumbs, or mix with your fingertips.

To make the filling, mix the blackberries and apples together and put into a deep 20 cm (8 inch) baking dish. Add a little water and the sugar, then mix thoroughly. Sprinkle the crumble mixture over the top and press down lightly with the back of a fork.

Bake in the oven at 190°C/375°F/mark 5 for 20 minutes or until the top of the crumble is lightly browned. Serve hot, warm or cold, with thick Greek yogurt or cream.

Serves 4–6

Elderberry and Apple Pie

Elderberry and apple pie is a treat for a September weekend, when the crop of elderberries is still flourishing in the late summer sun, and apples are plentiful. Elderberries have a unique, strong flavour which is very evocative of the turning year and berrying time. They are delicious when combined with apples and served with either thick cream or creamy Greek yogurt.

450 g (1 lb) cooking apples, peeled,
cored and thinly sliced

150 ml ($\frac{1}{4}$ pint/$\frac{2}{3}$ cup) dry cider

60 ml (4 tbsp/$\frac{1}{3}$ cup) clear honey

175 g (6 oz/1$\frac{1}{2}$ cups) elderberries,
stripped from their stalks

sweet crust pastry (see page 92)

beaten egg, to glaze

Put the apple slices in a bowl. Blend the cider and honey together in a pan over a low heat. Bring to simmering point and stir into the apples. Fold in the elderberries. Leave to cool.

Roll out two-thirds of the pastry and use to line an 18 cm (7 inch) pie dish that is at least 5 cm (2 inches) deep. Put in the apples and berries with some of the juices. Roll out the remaining pastry and use to cover the pie. Press the moistened pastry edges together with a fork. Brush the top with beaten egg.

Bake in the oven at 200°C/400°F/mark 6 for 30 minutes or until golden brown. Serve hot, with thick cream or Greek yogurt.

Serves 4–6

When elderberries appear, the farmer knows that it is time to sow winter wheat. 'With purple fruit when elder branches bend/ And their high hues the hips and cornets lend/Ere yet the chill hoar frost comes, or sleepy rain,/Sow with choice wheat the neatly furrowed plain.'

Blackberry and Apple Cake

Serve this moist, succulent cake as a delightful snack or a dessert with custard or cream.

175 g (6 oz/1½ cups) plain (all-purpose) flour
pinch of salt
100 g (4 oz/½ cup) sunflower margarine
75 g (3 oz/6 tbsp) caster (superfine) sugar
225 g (8 oz/1⅓ cups) blackberries, hulled
350 g (12 oz/3 cups) apples, cored and grated
3 eggs
caster (superfine) sugar, to dredge

Grease a 20 cm (8 inch) cake tin. Sift the flour with the salt into a bowl and rub in the margarine. Add the sugar and fruit. Stir in the eggs with a spoon. Do not beat. Put into the tin.

Bake in the oven at 180°C/350°F/mark 4 for 45–55 minutes until cooked through but still slightly moist in the centre. Dredge with caster (superfine) sugar while still warm.
Serves 6–8

These orchards that have lonely stood since spring,
Swelling their fruit unnoted in the sun,
Are populous suddenly, with ringing voice,
September mornings, when the sun's yet low,
And dew upon the leas
Make brambles glisten and the mushrooms grow.
Codlin's already stripped; his day was done
When August holidays were first begun,
Being the children's apple, earliest ripe
And nothing worth for keeping; only worth
Young teeth, and summer fun.
But Quarrendens, and Russets nicely browned,
And common Councillors, of varied stripe,
And Pippins smelling of the rainy earth
Wait to be harvested
With Peasgood Nonesuch, giant in his girth,
Cox, Blenheim, Ribstone, properly renowned,
Apples that wait for Christmas, darkly stored
On shelf or floor, not touching, one by one.

Vita Sackville-West: 'The Land'

BLACKBERRY
AND APPLE CAKE
(PAGE 102) WITH
BLACKBERRY
CRISP (PAGE 97)

Apple Strudel

Nothing can beat a freshly cooked apple strudel, the lightest of pastries. This recipe has all the freshness of the autumn crop of apples. As the Bramley apple tree on my lawn carries on producing ripe fruit through October, I make quantities of apple purée and use it for such goodies as this delicious strudel.

350 g (12 oz/3 cups) windfall apples, peeled, cored and chopped
75 g (3 oz/6 tbsp) caster (superfine) sugar
2.5 ml (½ tsp) ground cinnamon
50 g (2 oz/⅓ cup) raisins
40 g (1½ oz/⅓ cup) hazelnuts (filberts), chopped and toasted
25 g (1 oz/½ cup) fresh white breadcrumbs
2 large sheets filo pastry
25 g (1 oz/2 tbsp) butter, melted
icing (confectioners') sugar, to dust

Put the apples into a pan with a little water and cook to a pulp. Add the sugar and stir over a gentle heat, smoothing the purée with a wooden spoon. Add the cinnamon and raisins. Mix the nuts with the breadcrumbs.

Brush each sheet of filo with the melted butter. Arrange the apple purée along the shorter side of each piece of filo. Sprinkle the nut mixture over the top. Roll up carefully, folding in the edges like a parcel. Make two large strudel rolls in this way. Carefully transfer to a baking sheet and brush the pastry with the remaining melted butter.

Bake in the oven at 190°C/375°F/mark 5 for 20–25 minutes until golden and crisp. Cool.

To serve, cut each strudel into 4 long diagonal slices about 5 cm (2 inches) wide. Dust with sifted icing (confectioners') sugar.
Makes 8

Apple Upside-Down Cake

This is a lovely, gooey dessert that brings back memories of rich 'nursery' puddings before the days of calorie-counting. It is irresistible served fresh from the oven, with lashings of thick Greek yogurt.

200 g (7 oz/⅞ cup) butter
15–20 ml (1 heaped tbsp) brown sugar
450 g (1 lb) apples, peeled, cored and sliced
350 g (12 oz/3 cups) plain (all-purpose) flour
7.5 ml (1½ tsp) baking powder
pinch of salt
1 egg
100 g (4 oz/½ cup) caster (superfine) sugar
150 ml (¼ pint/⅔ cup) milk
a few drops of vanilla flavouring

Put 75 g (3 oz/6 tbsp) of the butter and the brown sugar into a 20 cm (8 inch) square deep cake tin and melt in the tin. Put the apple slices into the bottom of the tin on top of the butter and sugar mixture.

Sift the dry ingredients together. Melt the remaining butter over a gentle heat. Beat the egg with the sugar in a bowl until thick and pale, then mix in the milk. Add the dry ingredients to the mixture, then the melted butter and vanilla flavouring. Beat well. Spread the dough over the apple slices in the cake tin.

Bake in the oven at 180°C/350°F/mark 4 for 40 minutes. Leave to cool on a wire rack for 15 minutes. Run a knife around the side of the tin to loosen the cake and turn it over on to a warmed plate, leaving the cake tin over it for a few minutes to allow the syrup to soak in. Serve with plenty of cream or yogurt.
Serves 6–8

Apple Sponge

This recipe, with its light sponge topping, is a good alternative to apple crumble. It's lovely served warm with cream or custard.

450 g (1 lb) apples, peeled, cored and sliced
a little sugar
icing (confectioners') sugar, to dust
For the sponge topping
100 g (4 oz/½ cup) sunflower margarine
100 g (4 oz/½ cup) light brown sugar
2 eggs
225 g (8 oz/2 cups) plain (all-purpose) flour
7.5 ml (1½ tsp) baking powder
15 ml (1 tbsp) lemon juice
grated rind of ½ lemon

Put the apple slices into the bottom of a 20 cm (8 inch) cake tin, sprinkle with a little sugar and mix well.

To make the topping, cream the margarine with the sugar in a bowl, then beat in the eggs. Sift in the dry ingredients, beating all the time. Add the lemon juice and rind. Spread the mixture over the apples in the tin.

Bake in the oven at 180°C/350°F/mark 4 for 30 minutes. Serve hot or warm, dusted with icing (confectioners') sugar.
Serves 6

Apple Sauce Cake

This is one of my favourite ways of using up the apple purée that I make every year. The cake has a very special texture and is good as a dessert or with coffee or tea. You can use frozen purée, of course, so this is a cake for all seasons, which will recall golden September days of fallen apples among the turning leaves.

450 g (1 lb) cooking apples, peeled, cored and chopped
100 g (4 oz/½ cup) sunflower margarine
225 g (8 oz/1 cup) caster (superfine) sugar
1 egg
150 g (5 oz/1¼ cups) plain (all-purpose) flour
5 ml (1 tsp) ground allspice
5 ml (1 tsp) grated nutmeg
pinch of ground cloves
5 ml (1 tsp) baking powder
pinch of salt
For the icing (optional)
fresh lemon juice
icing (confectioners') sugar

Thoroughly grease a 20 cm (8 inch) cake tin. Put the apples with a little water in a pan and cook gently until mushy. Mash to a purée.

Cream the margarine with the sugar in a bowl, then beat in the egg. Stir in the apple purée. Sift the dry ingredients together and mix into the apple mixture. Put into the prepared tin.

Bake in the oven at 180°C/350°F/mark 4 for 25 minutes until a knife inserted into the centre comes out clean.

If liked, ice with lemon icing when cold. To make the icing, simply add fresh lemon juice to sifted icing (confectioners') sugar until a spreading consistency is obtained.
Serves 4–6

Windfall Cake

I have been making this apple cake for years, and it has never let me down. The cake is moist, fruity and extremely more-ish. You can enjoy it on its own, or serve it warmed, as a dessert, with thick yogurt or custard. Many a windfall has been mopped up in this way!

250 g (9 oz/2¼ cups) self raising (self-rising) flour
pinch of salt
175 g (6 oz/¾ cup) sunflower margarine
100 g (4 oz/½ cup) caster (superfine) sugar
100 g (4 oz/⅔ cup) sultanas (golden raisins)
350 g (12 oz/3 cups) windfall apples, weighed when peeled, cored and diced
2 eggs
caster (superfine) sugar, to dredge

Grease a 20 cm (8 inch) deep cake tin. Sift the flour with the salt into a bowl and rub in the margarine. Stir in the sugar, sultanas (golden raisins) and apples. Stir in the eggs with a spoon. Do not beat. Put the mixture into the prepared cake tin.

Bake in the oven at 180°C/350°F/mark 4 for 50 minutes until a skewer inserted into the centre comes out clean. Serve warm from the oven, dredged with caster (superfine) sugar.
Serves 8

And August comes, when fields are sere and brown,
When stubble takes the place of ruffling corn;
When the sweet grass is like a prisoner shorn;
The air is full of drifting thistledown,
Grey pointed sprites, that on the breezes ride.
The cloyed trees droop, the ash-keys spinning fall;
The brooks are pebbly, for the trickle's dried;
Birds moult, and in the leafy copses hide,
And summer makes a silence after spring,
As who with age a liberal youth should chide.

Vita Sackville-West: 'The Land'

WINDFALL CAKE
(THIS PAGE)

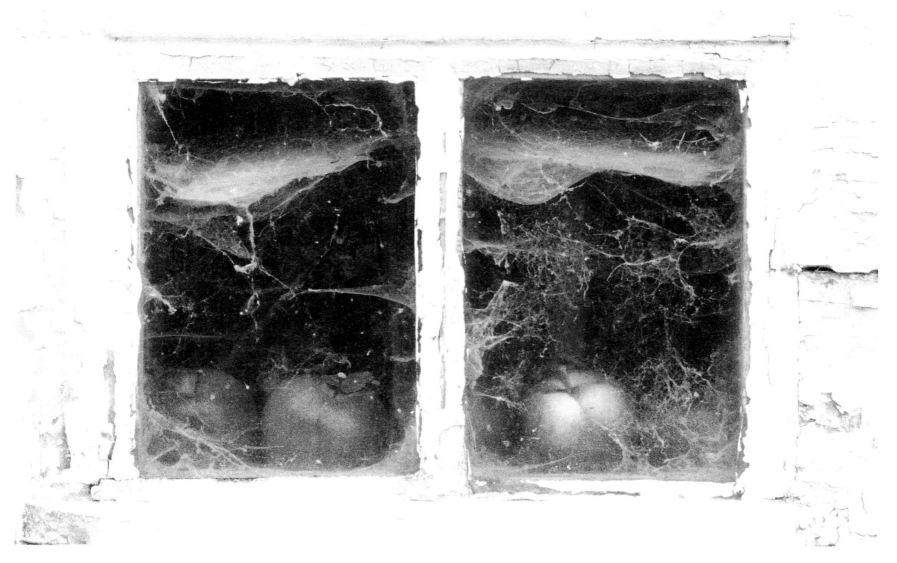

Apple Nut Turnovers

There are few autumnal apple treats more delect-able than these nourishing turnovers.

700 g (1½ lb) cooking apples (tart green apples),
peeled, cored and finely sliced

sugar, to taste

40 g (1½ oz/3 tbsp) sunflower margarine

40 g (1½ oz/¼ cup) candied peel

2.5 ml (½ tsp) ground cinnamon

30 ml (2 tbsp/3 tbsp) hazelnuts (filberts),
sliced and browned

1 egg yolk, beaten

caster (superfine) sugar, to sprinkle

Cook the apple slices in a little water and sugar to taste in a pan until mushy. Stir in the margarine, candied peel and cinnamon. Fold in the nuts.

Thinly roll out the pastry and cut into eight squares. Put 30 ml (2 tbsp) of the apple mixture in the centre, then fold the pastry over to make a triangle. Moisten the edges and press together with a fork. Make a small slit in the top of each turnover with a sharp knife. Brush with beaten egg yolk and sprinkle with caster sugar.

Bake in the oven at 200°C/400°F/mark 6 for 12–15 minutes until puffed and golden brown. Cool on a wire rack. Serve warm.

Makes 8 small turnovers

LEAVES, SEEDHEADS AND RUSHES

At the same time as the annual crop of apples is being harvested in garden and orchard, trees everywhere are turning autumnal colours – golds, bronzes, yellows, oranges, rusts, and reds of all kinds. The copper beech is in its full glory, and maples dazzle with their unbelievable hues. Late summer flowers have turned to seed, and a few rushes still stand on the banks of streams.

A walk in the countryside at this time of year, while the colours and fruits of autumn are at their height, is a pleasure in itself. It is also a good chance to collect some brilliantly coloured leaves, hips and haws, and a spray or two of hogweed (cow parsnip), for a seasonal arrangement. When you get home, arrange the bunch in a natural way, just as you would hold it. Put it into water in a big jug.

Leaves, seedheads and rushes make beautiful dried arrangements, capturing the moods of autumn. These can be used to cheer up the house through the coming winter.

Preserving Leaves with Glycerine

For preserving foliage, glycerining is a better method than air-drying because the leaves do not become brittle. Cut the branches of deciduous foliage in mid to late summer, well before it turns colour; evergreen foliage can be cut in early autumn. The leaves should be fresh and fully mature; dying leaves, and particularly those that have started to colour, will not absorb glycerine. Choose compact sprays rather than tall ones, to be sure that the glycerine will reach the uppermost leaves.

To help them absorb the glycerine fully, hammer the ends of woody branches, or split the ends of delicate stems with a sharp knife. Glycerine is very expensive, so remove any damaged or imperfect foliage from the branch or stem before preserving it. Preserve the leaves as soon as possible after picking; otherwise they will wilt and the chances of success will diminish accordingly.

Glycerine tends to turn the leaves brown, though some become gold, grey or nearly black. Glycerined leaves, however, remain supple and are easy to arrange, and the resulting shades are lovely in themselves. A few flowers are also suitable for preserving in glycerine; use the same method as for branches.

Use two parts boiling water to 1 part glycerine. Mix well, to prevent the heavier glycerine from settling on the bottom. Strip the bark from the base of the branch, and hammer the bottom 5 cm (2 inches). Use a tall, narrow, very stable container so that the stems are well supported.

Pour 7.5–10 cm (3–4 inches) glycerine solution into the pot, allowing the mixture to cool before inserting soft-stemmed material. Put the stems or branches in, and keep in a cool, dark place. Replace the glycerine as it is absorbed. The entire process takes from several days to six weeks or more; the smaller and thinner the leaves, the more quickly the process is complete. When they are ready, their colour will have changed evenly, and they will feel smooth and leathery.

If the leaves have absorbed too much glycerine, they will droop and/or ooze glycerine. To remedy this, gently clean the surfaces with warm, soapy water, and pat dry thoroughly.

If the uppermost leaves of a large branch have not been reached by the solution, they will wither. Wiping these leaves with glycerine several times during the course of preserving can sometimes remedy this. Thick leaves, such as eleagnus, also benefit from occasional wiping with glycerine.

You can also submerge whole leaves or sprays in a bath of equal parts glycerine and cold water. This method works well for large leaves preserved individually, such as mahonia and bergenia, and small, leathery leaves, such as ivy. Submerge them in the bath so that they do not overlap, and leave them – the timing varies,

as before, from several days to a month or more. Check regularly that the leaves remain fully submerged, and top up the solution as necessary. When ready, remove the leaves, wash gently and lay on newspaper to dry for a few days.

FOLIAGE FOR GLYCERINING
Bay (Laurus)
Beech (Fagus)
Berberis (evergreen species)
Bergenia
Birch (Betula)
Box (Buxus)
Butcher's broom (Ruscus)
Camellia
Eleagnus
Escallonia
Eucalyptus
False castor oil plant (Fatsia)
Hellebore (evergreen Helleborus species)
Hosta

Ivy (Hedera)
Laurel (evergreen Prunus species)
Magnolia (evergreen species)
Mahonia
Maple (Acer)
Mexican orange (Choisya)
Oak (Quercus)
Paeony (Paeonia)
Pittosporum
Privet (Ligustrum)
Rhododendron
Rosemary (Rosmarinus)
Spotted laurel (Aucuba)
Sweet chestnut (Castanea)
Whitebeam (*Sorbus aria*)
Viburnum (evergreen species)

FLOWERS FOR GLYCERINING
Bells of Ireland (Molucella)
Knotwort (Polygonum)
Lime (Tilia)
Masterwort (Astrantia)

ARRANGEMENTS WITH LEAVES, SEEDHEADS AND RUSHES

Let your arrangement of leaves and seedheads echo autumn's glorious abandon. Rich colours and contrasting textures can be combined to spectacular effect. Aim for natural, flowing lines, avoiding anything stiff, formal or self-conscious.

For example, use the shiny leaves of copper beech preserved in glycerine, with some soft, wispy wild clematis seedheads, which you can preserve by spraying with lacquer or hair spray. Poppy seedheads make an interesting contrast of texture, along with brittle honesty and the granular, rusty-red seedheads of dock. The softness of pampas grass and bulrush could add yet another pleasing texture.

Pressing Leaves

Pressing is an effective way of preserving foliage, especially leaves that have already turned colour. Though three-dimensionality is lost in pressing, colour and form are beautifully preserved. Choose unblemished, supple, dry leaves, newly fallen or still on the tree. (Thick or very sculptural leaves, such as holly, are unsuitable.) Place them in a single layer, and not overlapping, on newspaper, blotting paper or tissue. Cover them with another layer of the paper. Press under heavy books, bricks or heavy carpet in a warm room and leave for 3–4 weeks. Check after 2–3 days, and change the paper if it is damp. The longer it is pressed, the thinner the leaf becomes, and the more its original colour is retained. Store pressed leaves in layers, in a box in a dry room, otherwise the leaves can reabsorb moisture and then rot.

Later on in the autumn and early winter you can sometimes find skeletonized leaves of magnolia, camellia, holly, rhododendron or laurel underneath their respective trees or shrubs. These lacy, delicate leaves consist of only the midrib and veins, the softer epidermis having rotted away.

To skeletonize leaves the old-fashioned way, pick them while fresh, and soak them for two months in dirty rainwater. When the surface feels slippery, rub the green epidermis off with your fingers, then rinse. Soak in a mild solution of bleach for 1 hour, rinse again, pat dry, then press as above or in a flower press. Alternatively, boil them in 100 g (4 oz) household soda dissolved in 1 litre ($1\frac{3}{4}$ pints/$4\frac{1}{4}$ cups) water for 1 hour, then rub off the epidermis, and proceed as before. You can make very attractive greetings cards using skeletonized leaves, either in their natural state, or sprayed silver and glued on to cardboard.

LEAVES FOR PRESSING

Ash (Fraxinus)
Azalea (Rhododendron)
Beech (Fagus)
Blackberry (Rubus)
Boston ivy (Parthenocissus)
Cherry (Prunus)
Clematis
Epimedium
Ferns (various genera)
Foam flower (Tiarella)
Geranium
Gladiolus
Globe thistle (Echinops)
Grape (Vitis)
Honeysuckle (Lonicera)
Iris
Maidenhair (Ginkgo)
Maple (Acer)
Mullein (Verbascum)
Oak (Quercus)
Peach (Prunus)
Plum (Prunus)
Poplar (Populus)
Senecio 'Sunshine'
Silverdust (*Cineraria maritima*)
Smoke bush (Cotinus)
Sumach (Rhus)
Sweet chestnut (Castanea)
Virginia creeper (Parthenocissus)
Whitebeam (Sorbus)

A STILL LIFE

Coloured leaves, pine cones, wild clematis, fresh fruit or gourds, nuts, a pineapple, some teazels or an artichoke, a sunflower, skeletonized leaves can be piled up artistically on a large patterned platter or in a shallow urn. Place on top of a painted chest, or cover a plain chest or table with a patterned rug and put the arrangement there; or it could look lovely in front of a painting.

You could make a wall arrangement with a sculptured effect, like a delicate wood carving. Twine a hop-bine around bamboo or wire according to the shape you want. Fill inside this outline with wild clematis, honesty, dried cones or seedheads so that the colours are all natural browns, creams and white.

Preserving Grasses

Grasses dry well, and they add both lightness and height to a dried flower arrangement. Some grasses can be picked at several stages: when in flower, when the seeds have set but are green and unripe, and when fully ripe. As grasses are plentiful, you can experiment freely. Handle fully ripe grasses with care, as they are liable to disintegrate. A light fixative spray often helps. Air-dry grasses either spread flat or upright in full containers. With the latter method, slender-stemmed grasses often dry in graceful, arching curves. Drying the leaves as well as the stems is useful for creating natural-looking displays.

GRASSES FOR AIR-DRYING
Animated oat (Avena)
Bent grass (Agrostis)
Canary grass (Phalaris)
Cloud grass (Agrostis)
Cocksfoot grass (Dactylis)
Feather grass (Stipa)
Fountain grass (Pennisetum)
Hare's tail grass (Lagurus)
Lesser and greater quaking grass
Meadow foxtail (Alopecurus)

Pampas grass (Cortaderia)
Pearl grass (Briza)
Ruby grass (Tricholaena)
Silver grass (Miscanthus)
Squirrel-tail grass (Hordeum)
Wheat (Triticum)
Wild barley (Hordeum)

Preserving Bulrushes and Pampas Grass

Bulrushes (less commonly known as cat-tail or reedmace) and pampas grass should be picked before they reach full maturity: July or August for bulrushes, September for pampas grass. Bulrushes are at their best for picking when the golden tassels of male flowers, on the upper part of the stem, are still in bloom. Pick pampas grass as the plumes protrude from the tops of the stems, but before becoming fluffy, since they continue maturing as they dry. Air-dry upright in a tall container. Once dry, they can be sprayed lightly with hair lacquer or fixative.

The woodland swamps with mosses varified
And bullrush forrests bowing by the side
Of shagroot sallows that snug shelter make
For the coy morehen in her bushy lake
Into whose tide a little runnel weaves
Such charms for silence through the choaking leaves
A whimpling melodys that but intrude
As lullabys to ancient solitude
The wood grass plats which last year left behind
Weaving their feathery lightness to the wind
Look now as picturesque amid the scene
As when the summer glossed their stems in green
While hasty hare brunts through the creepy gap
Seeks the soft beds and squats in safetys lap

John Clare: 'Word Pictures in Winter'

Capturing the Flavour of Autumn

The autumn colours are fleeting. They must be captured at the moment of their peak, for suddenly they are gone, the colour faded, the leaf fallen. The harvest of berries, too, goes over the top into over-ripeness and decay. Every year varies with the weather, although country lore would advise us to gather blackberries before Michaelmas Day in mid-October! Nonetheless, it is worth making the most of the berries while they are at their most delicious. They don't all have to be eaten there and then: you can make wonderful drinks and cordials for the weeks ahead, and sensational concoctions for Christmas.

CHAPTER THREE

Cordials, Country Wines and Teas

The trees in wood and hedgerow are yellowing. Dying leaves flutter to the ground in the damp autumn chill, as October merges into November. Fluffy, cloud-coloured seedhead of the wild clematis is barely visible in the morning mists. As the sun struggles through it catches the gold of the beech standing in frosted, drooping grass. Cobwebs hang suspended across dying hollyhocks, their tracery outlined by frozen dewdrops, filigree silver. Heavy-berried hawthorn hangs silent as the white hoar frost dissolves to a crystal day.

Late autumn often brings these diamond days: clear, pure light, cold but brilliant, the low sun glinting on the gilded trees. Leaves of ash are silhouetted against the sky by the almost horizontal sun; plough furrows are etched in lines of light between lines of dark shadow. Dead hay-coloured grasses in the hedge-bottom are tinged with gold, and ivy is coming into creamy flower.

A pool of bright scarlet yew berries has fallen under the tree, staining the bare ground like blood. Rosehips look even brighter on their bare branches. The last of the elderberries hang on limp, slender stalks. As morning progresses a damp chill rises from the wet grass, and only the sound of dripping is heard in the stillness. The birds that remain find nothing to sing about: a lonely robin hops hopefully around the garden, resting on the spade handle and puffing out his feathers in an attempt to get himself warm.

The autumn harvest is drawing towards its end. The garden is a scene of glorious untidiness as everything dies back, as yet unready to be cut down and burned. There is a beauty in this untidiness, the beauty of abundance and abandon. Windfall apples still cover the grass under the tree, falling daily into the dead leaves. Walnuts lie hidden among the damp leaves too, and the very last of the blackberries are waiting to be harvested. The sloe, late to come into fruit, is ripening on its thorny bush, hard little bluish fruits with a dusky bloom. They only taste right after the first frost.

Rippling shadows of branches outside the kitchen window slant through on the low sunlight as the cooking activity continues. It is time to make fresh fruit drinks and cordials that capture the essence of autumn's flavours; sloe gin and other alcoholic concoctions to celebrate Christmas and special occasions; and home-made wine from country fruits and garden produce. Reaping and gleaning the annual harvest to its full in the mellow days of the turning year.

GRAPE CORDIAL
(PAGE 121)

CORDIALS AND OTHER FRUIT DRINKS

Cordials are highly flavoured, aromatic drinks. Strong and sweet, many of them were originally developed for medicinal purposes, but they are delightful in their own right. Many fruits — including berries, grapes, sloes, plums, apples and crab apples — make delicious drinks, alcoholic or non-alcoholic. Use them for a celebration or just to warm up a cold winter's night.

Blackberry Cordial for Christmas

This dark, rich, smooth liqueur, with the tang of Christmas, is one of the best I have ever tasted.

900 g (2 lb) blackberries, hulled
450 g (1 lb/2 cups) granulated sugar
¼ whole nutmeg
25 g (1 oz/¼ cup) whole cloves
15 g (½ oz) cinnamon stick
300 ml (½ pint/1¼ cups) brandy

Put the blackberries into a food processor or blender with a little of the sugar. Blend to a purée, then sieve. Put the purée into a pan with the sugar and spices. Cover and simmer gently for 20 minutes. Cool a little, then add the brandy.

Bottle and set aside for Christmas. Strain the cordial before using. Drink it in tot-size glasses.
Makes 900 ml (1½ pints/3¾ cups)

Then comes the harvest supper night
Which rustics welcome with delight
When merry game and tiresome tale
And songs increasing with the ale
Their mingled uproar interpose
To crown the harvests happy close
While rural mirth that there abides
Laughs till she almost cracks her sides

John Clare: 'The Shepherd's Calendar'

BLACKBERRY
CORDIAL FOR
CHRISTMAS
(PAGE 118),
BLACKBERRY
VODKA
(PAGE 121), WILD
PLUM VODKA
(PAGE 124)

Blackberry Quencher

This simple recipe makes one of the best fresh fruit drinks of the autumn. It doesn't keep for long, so be sure to make the most of the blackberry harvest while it lasts!

900 g (2 lb) blackberries
100 g (4 oz/½ cup) granulated sugar
900 ml (1½ pints/3¾ cups) bottled mineral water

Purée the fruit and sugar in a food processor or blender. Strain through a sieve to separate the pulp from the pips. Stir in the water.

Bottle. Store in the refrigerator for a few days, or freeze. Dilute to drink with sparkling mineral water.
Makes 1.4 litres (2½ pints/6¼ cups)

Blackberry Cocktail

Blackberries and vodka are an excellent combination, and this blackberry cocktail makes a special and original drink — it's like velvet and fire simultaneously.

blackberries
sugar to taste
vodka

Purée the blackberries with sugar to taste in a blender or food processor.

Sieve the puréed blackberries in order to separate the pulp from the pips. Add the blackberry purée to half that quantity of vodka and you have a delicious cocktail — sister to a Bloody Mary and even more delicious.

Blackberry Vodka

Blackberries surrender their exquisite flavour to vodka and stain it a deep dark red, almost black. Blackberry vodka makes a wonderful liqueur and a celebration tot.

450 g (1 lb) blackberries, hulled
100 g (4 oz/½ cup) granulated sugar
10 whole, unpeeled almonds
1.1 litres (2 pints/5 cups) vodka

Drop the blackberries into a clean bottle until they reach two-thirds of the way up. Pour the sugar over the top of them through a funnel. Bruise the almonds by tapping with a meat hammer or rolling pin. Add them to the blackberries, then pour in the vodka. Shake the bottle.

Shake daily for a few days until the sugar has completely dissolved. Leave for 3 months, then strain off into another bottle. Seal tightly. Store for 1 year before drinking.
Makes 1.4 litres (2½ pints/6¼ cups)

Raspberry Nectar

A late crop of autumn raspberries makes a delicious fruit drink if you have already made enough jam and Raspberry Sauce (page 153) to see you through the winter! This is truly lovely – the flavour of raspberries and orange, sweetened with honey, is indeed nectar.

450 g (1 lb) raspberries, hulled
45 ml (3 tbsp/4 tbsp) clear honey
5 ml (1 tsp) lemon juice
juice of 2 oranges
600 ml (1 pint/2½ cups) bottled mineral water

Blend the raspberries with the honey and fruit juices in a food processor or blender. Press through a sieve, extracting as much of the juice as possible. Add the water.

Store in the refrigerator for a few days – or freeze. Serve diluted with sparkling mineral water and a sprig of mint floating on top.
Makes 1.1 litres (2 pints/5 cups)

Grape Cordial

The subtle flavour of grape juice, highlighted with lemon, makes a lovely cordial. And it looks as wonderful as it tastes.

juice of 2 lemons
50 g (2 oz/scant ½ cup) icing (confectioners') sugar
1.8 kg (4 lb) ripe grapes
600 ml (1 pint/2½ cups) sparkling mineral water, chilled
fresh fruit, such as sliced oranges, strawberries, and limes, whole mulberries and blackberries, peeled and halved grapes
mint sprigs, to decorate
crushed ice, to serve

Mix the lemon juice with the sugar to a smooth paste and add to the grapes. Purée the grapes in a blender. Strain the purée or put through a fruit juice extractor.

Put the grape cordial into a pretty bowl or jug with the chilled mineral water. Float the fruit in the cordial. Decorate with mint sprigs.

To serve, put some crushed ice into the bottom of a tall glass and top up with the grape cordial, some of the fruit and a sprig of mint. Grape cordial keeps in the refrigerator for several days.
Makes 1.7 litres (3 pints/7½ cups)

Hot Elderberry Juice

This is an old fashioned remedy for coughs, colds, sore throats, sciatica and neuralgia.

600 ml (1 pint/2½ cups) elderberry juice (see method)
225 g (8 oz/1 cup) granulated sugar

Wash and drain the berries. Heat slowly in a stone or earthenware jar, covered with a lid, in the oven at 110°C/225°F/mark ¼ for several hours or overnight. Drain.

Simmer 600 ml (1 pint/2½ cups) juice with the sugar for 30 minutes until a quarter of the juice has evaporated. Pour into a clean bottle and seal.
Makes about 450 ml (¾ pint/2 cups)

Elderberry juice was used in country medicine as a cure for all ills. There is a 16th century slimming cure recommended by John Gerard, the herbalist: 'The seeds contained within the berries dried are good for such as have the dropsie, and such as are too fat, and would faine be leaner, if they be taken in a morning to the quantity of a dram with wine for a certain space.'

Sloe Gin

Sloe-ing is an annual expedition for my family, after the first frost, when the fruits have developed their full flavour. The resulting Sloe Gin, a beautiful dark pink colour, is a warming drink on dismal winter evenings. If you allow it to mature for one year, it will taste even better. (To put the gin-soaked sloes to good use after you strain off the liquid, see Sloe Brandy, below).

10 whole almonds
450 g (1 lb) sloes
100 g (4 oz/½ cup) granulated sugar
900 ml (1½ pints/3¾ cups) gin

Bruise the almonds by tapping with a meat hammer or rolling pin. Wash, dry and prick the sloes with a sharp knife. Put them into a bottle, then add the sugar and almonds. Pour in the gin through a funnel, then put a top on the bottle. Shake well. Shake every day for 1–2 weeks, then store for at least 3 months.

Strain the gin off the sloes and decant into a clean bottle. If possible, allow to mature for 1 year before drinking.
Makes 900 ml (1½ pints/3¾ cups)

Sloe Brandy

It seems a pity to throw away the gin-soaked sloes you have used when making Sloe Gin, so try this idea. Just adding brandy and a little sugar makes a powerful and fiery tot.

175 g (6 oz/1½ cups) gin-soaked sloes
(see Sloe Gin, above)
75 g (3 oz/6 tbsp) granulated sugar
450 ml (¾ pint/2 cups) brandy

Put the soaked sloes into a bottle and add the sugar through a funnel. Pour in the brandy to cover the fruit. Seal the bottle.

Shake well daily until the sugar has dissolved. Leave to stand for 1 month before drinking, then strain.
Makes about 600 ml (1 pint/2½ cups)

Blackberry Rob

This thick blackberry drink used to be given as a traditional remedy for colds – pleasant medicine indeed. A warming and nourishing drink with the flavour of autumn, it is delicious with soda water and ice.

900 g (2 lb) blackberries, hulled
a little sugar
8 cloves
1 cinnamon stick
100 g (4 oz/½ cup) brown sugar

Purée the blackberries with a little sugar in a blender. Sieve to separate the pulp from the pips. Add the spices and brown sugar and simmer until thick and syrupy. Cool, then bottle. Serve chilled, strained to remove the spices.
Makes about 600 ml (1 pint/2½ cups)

Pear and Orange Cordial

Pear with orange makes a happy combination, and as a drink this is really delicious. Use juicy pears – I make full use of my crop of Williams for this recipe. Store the cordial in the refrigerator, where it will keep for about a month. It is lovely served on crushed ice, with a sprig of mint.

900 g (2 lb) ripe pears, chopped
grated rind and juice of 4 large oranges
225 g (8 oz/1 cup) granulated sugar
900 ml (1½ pints/3¾ cups) water
15 g (½ oz) citric acid

Put the pears in a large pan and cover with water. Simmer until the fruit is soft. Strain through a jelly bag or a clean linen tea towel.

Combine the pear and orange juices. Put into the cleaned pan with the orange rind, sugar and water. Heat gently until the sugar has dissolved, stirring all the time. Cool a little, then stir in the citric acid. Bottle.
Makes 1.1 litres (2 pints/5 cups)

In order to make a sick child better, the child would be passed through an arch of bramble that had rooted at both ends. If the following verse was recited at the same time, it would cure the child of the whooping cough: 'In bramble, out cough, Here I leave the whooping cough.'

Plum Cordial

This very simple fruit drink is delicious during the autumn – it does not keep for longer than 2 months so it is a seasonal drink. Some years, my neighbour's plum trees look as if they will break under the weight of all the fruit. The branches hang down burdened with ripe, purplish-red plums, and this is an excellent way of using them.

900 g (2 lb) plums, stoned and chopped
350 g (12 oz/1½ cups) granulated sugar
600 ml (1 pint/2½ cups) water
15 g (½ oz) citric acid

Cook the plums with the sugar and water in a pan for about 20 minutes until soft.

Purée in a blender and strain through a sieve. Stir in the citric acid. Bottle. Dilute to drink.
Makes 1.1 litres (2 pints/5 cups)

PLUM CORDIAL
(THIS PAGE)

Apple Juice

As October advances, the leaves in the garden start to turn colour and fall; early morning mists shroud the silent land. Each day under my apple tree, I find a new batch of windfalls in the long grass around the trunk. Home-made apple juice is an excellent recipe for families with children – they love it.

1.8 kg (4 lb) windfall apples
275 g (10 oz/1¼ cups) granulated sugar

Chop up the apples coarsely, discarding any damaged parts. Put into a large pan and cover with water. Simmer until the fruit is pulpy.

Strain through a clean linen tea towel or jelly bag for several hours. Add sugar to taste while it is still warm, and stir until dissolved. Squeeze the bag from time to time to extract all the juices. Bottle in screwtop bottles. Dilute if desired with soda water. Apple juice can be stored in the refrigerator for a few days.
Makes 2.3 litres (4 pints/10 cups)

Wild Plum Vodka

Bullaces or damsons soaked in vodka give both their colour and their flavour to the alcohol and make a fruity, golden liqueur which tastes of the country. It is a fine drink, original and different.

450 g (1 lb) wild plums (bullaces or damsons),
halved and stoned
100 g (4 oz/½ cup) granulated sugar
1.1 litres (2 pints/5 cups) vodka

Put the bullaces into a large, clean bottle and add the sugar through a funnel. Add the vodka, seal the bottle and shake well. Continue to shake daily until the sugar has thoroughly dissolved and the vodka takes on the colour of the fruit.

Store in a cool, dark place for 3 months. Strain off the fruit, pour the vodka into a clean bottle and seal tightly. For best results, store for 1 year before drinking.
Makes 1.4 litres (2½ pints/6¼ cups)

In parts of France villagers used to bring apples and medlars to church on All Saints' Day, November 1st, as an offering to the souls of the departed. After mass they were sold off to pay for Masses for the Dead on All Souls' Day.

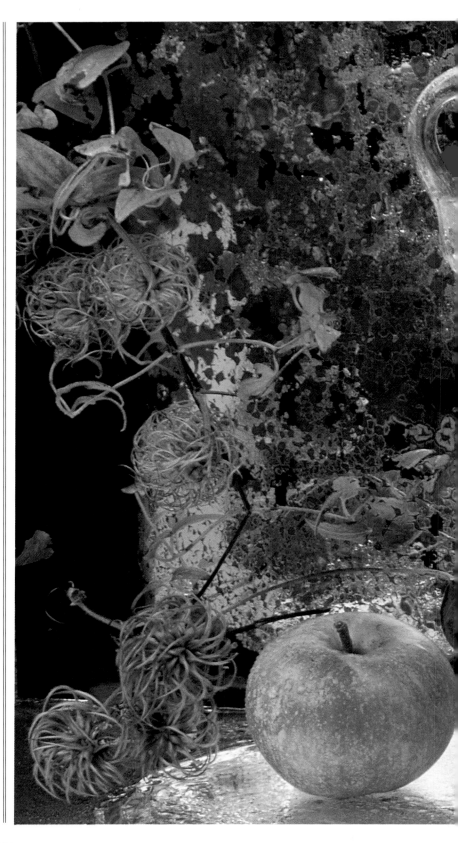

APPLE JUICE
(PAGE 124)

WINES FROM HEDGEROW AND GARDEN PRODUCE

People have been making country wines for centuries. There are as many methods for making home-made wine as there are wine-making enthusiasts. As in cooking food, these are based on personal experience. The recipes here have been recommended by friends, who all make lovely wines from hedgerow and garden produce.

GENERAL RULES

Wine is made by fermenting a sweet, flavoured liquid. Fermentation turns the natural sugar in fruit, vegetables or flowers, along with added sugar, into alcohol. First, activated yeast and some of the sugar are added to the fruit pulp and water, and allowed to ferment in a bucket. After the initial, vigorous fermentation, the 'must', as it is called, is strained into a glass demijohn, or fermentation jar, for further fermentation. An airlock allows the carbon dioxide to escape but prevents oxygen and air-borne bacteria from entering. The remaining sugar is added gradually during this time. After fermentation has ceased the wine is 'racked', or siphoned off the sediment, at intervals, and stored in a cool place. When it is very clear it is bottled.

To ensure that you make the most of your time and effort, and ingredients, keep in mind the following rules.

Cleanliness: Always ensure that pans, bowls, bottles, wooden spoons and other equipment are scrupulously clean. After washing, soak them in a sterilizing solution of 1 Campden (sterilizing) tablet dissolved in 300 ml ($\frac{1}{2}$ pint/$1\frac{1}{4}$ cups) water. For perfection, wash the fruit in this solution too, before using it.

Temperature: To ferment, wine needs a constant, even temperature, about 20–23°C/68–74°F. A warm kitchen or an airing cupboard is ideal.

Patience: Having gone to all the trouble of making your wine, give it a chance to mature fully before drinking – it is worth it. In general,

you should leave white wine for at least 6 months, and red wine for a year or two. The exact time will of course depend on the wine.

EQUIPMENT

Although wine-making equipment is specialized, it can be used for years to come. Here are the basics of what you will need.
Lidded plastic bucket
Strainer (cloth or nylon – never use anything metallic in the brewing process)
Sterilized bottle for stirring and crushing fruit
4.5 litre (1 gallon/5 quart) glass fermentation jars
1 m (3 feet) of rubber or plastic tubing, 5 mm ($\frac{1}{4}$ inch) in diameter
Campden (sterilizing) tablets
Wine bottles, new corks, labels and a wine rack
Yeast: for beginners, fresh or dried bakers' yeast

Blackberry Wine

This makes a dry, light red table wine. Serve it with red meats and cheese dishes.

1.8 kg (4 lb) blackberries, hulled
3.4 litres (6 pints/$3\frac{3}{4}$ quarts) boiling water
1 kg ($2\frac{1}{4}$ lb/$4\frac{1}{2}$ cups) granulated sugar
5 ml (1 tsp) citric acid
1 sachet wine yeast
1 Campden (sterilizing) tablet, crushed

Crush the blackberries in a bowl and pour the boiling water over them. Cover and leave to cool. Stir in the sugar, acid and yeast. Cover and leave to ferment on the pulp for 4 days, pressing down the floating fruit twice a day.

Strain, press dry and discard the fruit. Pour the liquid into a fermentation jar. Fit an airlock and put in a warm place until the wine is still and beginning to clear, about 2 weeks.

Rack the wine into a clean jar and top up with boiled, cooled water. Add the Campden (sterilizing) tablet. Bung it tightly, then leave in a cool place until the wine is bright. Bottle and store for at least 1 year.
Makes 6 bottles

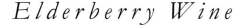

Wild Plum Wine

Wild plum wine can be made with bullaces of any variety, or with damsons. Both make a fruity table wine.

1.8 kg (4 lb) wild plums (bullaces or damsons), stalks removed
4.5 litres (1 gallon/5 quarts) boiling water
15 ml (1 tbsp) pectin enzyme
25 g (1 oz) fresh baker's yeast
(1 cake compressed yeast)
25 g (1 oz) yeast nutrient
1.4 kg (3 lb/6 cups) granulated sugar
225 g (8 oz/1⅓ cups) raisins

Put the bullaces into a plastic bucket. Pour the boiling water over them. When cool, add the pectin enzyme, stir well and cover. Leave to stand for 24 hours.

Add the yeast and nutrient. Cover and leave for 4 days, stirring daily. Strain the liquid on to the sugar, stirring well. Cover and keep in a warm place for 1 week. Pour into a fermentation jar. Fit an airlock and put in a warm place to ferment to a finish. Rack when the wine is clear. Leave to mature for 6 months before bottling.
Makes 6 bottles

Here the industrious huswives wend their way
Pulling the brittle branches carefull down
And hawking loads of berrys to the town
Wi unpretending skill yet half divine
To press and make their eldern berry wine
That bottld up becomes a rousing charm
To kindle winters icy bosom warm
That wi its merry partner nut brown beer
Makes up the peasants christmass keeping cheer

John Clare: 'The Shepherd's Calendar'

At one time it was believed that if you brought elder into the house you would bring the Devil too. In some areas it is called devil's wood. It is unlucky to burn elder wood in your house, or to make furniture from it. Elder wood was never used in ship-building because it was thought to be so unlucky.

Elderberry Wine

Elderberries make one of the finest hedgerow wines. Dark and full-bodied, it is best drunk when mature. Elderberries also make an excellent wine when combined with apples, blackberries or any of the wild plums. Pick the berries on a fine day.

2.3 kg (5 lb) elderberries, stripped off their stalks
4.5 litres (1 gallon/5 quarts) boiling water
thinly pared rind and juice of 1 lemon
50 g (2 oz) fresh root ginger
1.6 kg (3½ lb/7 cups) granulated sugar
20 g (¾ oz) fresh baker's yeast
(¾ cake compressed yeast)

Put the elderberries into a large bowl. Pour the boiling water over them, stirring with a spoon. Crush them slightly to release some of the juices. Cover with muslin (cheesecloth) and leave to stand for 3 days, stirring daily.

Strain off the juices into a pan with the thinly pared lemon rind. Bruise the ginger by tapping with a meat hammer or rolling pin to separate the fibres. Add it to the pan. Bring to the boil and simmer for 10 minutes. Allow to cool.

Put the sugar into a large bowl, pour the liquid over the top and stir well. Add the lemon juice. Cream the yeast with a little of the liquid. Leave for 5 minutes to ferment, then add to the liquid. Leave to ferment in a warm place for 3–4 days, still covered.

Strain the liquid into a fermentation jar until it is two-thirds full, then shake well. Fit an airlock and put in a warm place to ferment to a finish, about 3 months. Rack and bottle.

Elderberry wine is at its best after it has matured for a year or more. Store in a cool place at an even temperature.
Makes 6 bottles

Bilberry or Blueberry Wine

This wine is so good that country people used to call the bilberry the 'wine berry'. It makes a first-rate red table wine. Blueberries can be used instead – blueberry wine will have a bluish tinge initially, but this gradually disappears as the wine clears in the jar. You can also make grape wine using this recipe.

1.4 kg (3 lb) bilberries (or blueberries)
2.3 litres (4 pints/2½ quarts) boiling water
20 g (¾ oz) fresh baker's yeast
(¾ cake compressed yeast)
1.1 kg (2½ lb/5 cups) granulated sugar
30 ml (2 tbsp/3 tbsp) lemon juice

Put the bilberries or blueberries into a bowl. Pour the boiling water over them, stirring. Cover with muslin (cheesecloth) and leave to stand for 24 hours. Stir from time to time with a clean spoon or sterilized bottle, and press the fruit to extract some of the fruit juices.

Mix the yeast with 10 ml (2 tsp) of the sugar and 150 ml (¼ pint/⅔ cup) of the liquid. Leave for 5 minutes to ferment, then add to the mixture with the lemon juice and half of the sugar. Leave to ferment on the pulp for 3 days.

Strain the liquid into a fermentation jar, add the rest of the sugar so that the jar is two-thirds full, then shake well. Fit an airlock and put in a warm place to ferment to a finish, about 3 months. Rack the wine thoroughly before bottling.

Keep the wine for at least 6 months before drinking. Store in a cool place at an even temperature.
Makes 5 bottles

You could be forgiven for thinking that Wilding, Scrab, Gribble and Scrogg were a troupe of clowns or perhaps hobgoblins. They are, in fact, affectionate country names for the wild apple, or crab apple tree.

Crab Apple Wine

For this medium-sweet wine, pick the crab apples when they are really ripe.

1 kg (2¼ lb) crab apples, chopped
225 g (8 oz/2⅔ cups) cooking apples, grated
2.3 litres (4 pints/2½ quarts) boiling water
1.4 kg (3 lb/6 cups) granulated sugar
grated rind and juice of 1 lemon
grated rind and juice of 1 orange
25 g (1 oz) fresh bakers' yeast
(1 cake compressed yeast)

Crush the crab apples. Put the crab apples and grated apple into a plastic bucket. Pour the boiling water over them. Leave to cool. Mash. Leave to stand for 3 days, stirring daily.

Strain through a wine bag into a fermentation jar. Heat the sugar in 900 ml (1½ pints/3¾ cups) water to make a syrup. Pour the syrup into the jar with the fruit rinds and juices.

Cream the yeast with a little of the liquid, leave to ferment, then add to the jar. Make up the liquid with boiled, cooled water. Fit an airlock and put in a warm place to ferment to a finish, about 4 months. Rack and leave for a further 3 months. Bottle.
Makes 6 bottles

Next shall you reap your corn. Your oats shall fall
Before full ripeness set them on to shed,
But leave your barley till it droop the head
With ripened beard. The tall
Wheat for an early cut; at midday, walk
When sun is hot and high, and if you hear
Straw crackle in the standing crop,
And see the slender forest of the stalk
Still green towards the ground, but gold at top,
Then you may know that cutting-time is near.
Peas are pernickety; cut when you may.
Beans, the sweet-scented beans of spring, shall stand
Till pods are turning black, or till you clear
Against the needs of autumn for your land.

Vita Sackville-West: 'The Land'

Rosehip Wine

This is a hedgerow wine which improves with keeping. It is dry with a distinctive flavour. Pick the rosehips after the first frost.

1 kg (2¼ lb) rosehips
4.5 litres (1 gallon/5 quarts) boiling water
1 kg (2¼ lb/4½ cups) granulated sugar
juice of 1 lemon
juice of 1 orange
15 g (½ oz) fresh baker's yeast
(½ cake compressed yeast)

Mince the rosehips roughly in a food processor or by hand. Put into a plastic bucket and pour the boiling water over them. Stir with a long-handled clean wooden spoon. Leave to stand for 3 days, stirring daily. Strain through a wine bag.

Heat the sugar with the fruit juices to make a syrup. Add the syrup to the wine juice and pour into a fermentation jar.

Cream the yeast with a little of the liquid, leave to ferment, then add to the wine. Make up the amount of liquid to within 2.5 cm (1 inch) of the top of the jar with more boiled, cooled water. Fit an airlock and put in a warm place to ferment.

Rack into a clean jar and leave for a further 3 months at least. It will improve as it matures. Bottle.

Makes 6 bottles

Pumpkin Wine

This is an unusual and exotic way of using pumpkin. Melon wine can also be made successfully using this method.

2.3 kg (5 lb) ripe pumpkin, peeled and sliced
25 g (1 oz) fresh root ginger
4.5 litres (1 gallon/5 quarts) cold water
1 Campden (sterilizing) tablet, crushed
5 ml (1 tsp) pectin enzyme
1.4 kg (3 lb/6 cups) granulated sugar
wine yeast and nutrient
juice of 2 lemons

Put the pumpkin into a plastic bucket. Bruise the ginger by tapping with a meat hammer or rolling pin to separate the fibres. Add to the bucket, and cover with 3.4 litres (6 pints/3¾ quarts) of the cold water. Stir in the crushed Campden (sterilizing) tablet and pectin enzyme. Leave to stand for 24 hours.

Bring a further 1.1 litres (2 pints/5 cups) water to the boil. Add the sugar and stir until dissolved. Cool to blood heat, then add the pumpkin together with the yeast and nutrient and the lemon juice. Cover and leave to ferment in a warm place for 5 days, stirring twice daily.

Strain the liquid off the pulp into a fermentation jar. Fit an airlock and put in a warm place to ferment. Rack when the wine begins to clear.

Bottle when the fermentation has ended and the wine has cleared. Store in a cool place at an even temperature for at least 6 months before drinking.
Makes 6 bottles

Rowan Berry Wine

The rowan berry – the fruit of the rowan, or mountain ash, tree – is said to be good for sore throats, but any medicinal merits are matched by its quality as a good dry table wine. Allow it to mature well before drinking. Pick berries when they are ripe; some say you should allow them to ripen further after picking to prevent bitterness.

1 kg (2¼ lb) rowan berries, stalks removed
2.3 litres (4 pints/2½ quarts) boiling water
1.4 kg (3 lb/6 cups) granulated sugar
grated rind and juice of 2 oranges
10 ml (2 tsp) dried yeast

Put the rowan berries into a plastic bucket. Pour the boiling water over them. Leave to stand for 3 days, stirring daily. Strain through a wine bag into a fermentation jar.

Heat the sugar in 900 ml (1½ pints/3¾ cups) water to make a syrup. Pour the syrup into the jar with the orange rind and juice.

Cream the yeast with a little of the liquid, leave to ferment, then add to the wine. Put a cotton wool (cotton) bung into the neck of the jar and leave for 3 days. Fit an airlock and put in a warm place to ferment to a finish, about 4 months.

Rack into a clean jar and leave for at least 6 months. Bottle.
Makes 6 bottles

Hedgerow Wine

Blackberries, elderberries and plums combine here to make a fruity red table wine that tastes of no one fruit in particular. It has a beautiful colour, and will become very mellow with time.

1.4 kg (3 lb/6 cups) sugar
1.8 kg (4 lb) blackberries
1.8 kg (4 lb) elderberries
450 g (1 lb) plums
4.5 litres (1 gallon/5 quarts) water
40 g (1½ oz) yeast

Mix all the fruit together and boil for 30 minutes in the water. Strain into a pan and add the yeast when cool. Leave to stand for 10 days, stirring well every day. Strain into a fermentation jar, fit an airlock and leave to ferment to a finish. If liked, add a few raisins. Rack after 1 month, and bottle when clear.
Makes 6 bottles

HOME-MADE TEAS

Infusions made from the fresh or dried leaves, seeds and berries of hedgerow plants make refreshing drinks which can have considerable tonic value. They have been used by country folk for centuries. Some of the plants, with their undeniable properties, are commonly found in conventional medicine – dill and rosehip being two outstanding examples.

Home-made teas are made in a teapot and are very simple to prepare. You will be rewarded by the lovely aromas and delicious tastes of these natural brews.

DRYING LEAVES, SEEDS OR BERRIES

Strip leaves, seeds or berries off their stalks, and lay them on newspaper. Put them flat in a warm dry place, such as an airing cupboard, for 2–3 days, turning them occasionally, until brittle. Store in airtight jars in a cool dark place.

Dill Tea

Dill has a reputation for helping to cure insomnia, hiccups and nausea.

300 ml ($\frac{1}{2}$ pint/$1\frac{1}{4}$ cups) boiling water
5 ml (1 tsp) dill seeds, crushed in a mortar

Pour the boiling water over the crushed dill seeds in a teapot. Cover and infuse for 20 minutes. Strain.
Makes 300 ml ($\frac{1}{2}$ pint/$1\frac{1}{4}$ cups)

Fennel Tea

This tea is said to relieve catarrh, reduce weight and improve the eyesight as well as helping cure insomnia, hiccups and nausea.

300 ml ($\frac{1}{2}$ pint/$1\frac{1}{4}$ cups) boiling water
5 ml (1 tsp) fennel seeds, crushed in a mortar

Pour the boiling water over the crushed fennel seeds in a teapot. Cover and infuse for 20 minutes. Strain.
Makes 300 ml ($\frac{1}{2}$ pint/$1\frac{1}{4}$ cups)

Juniper Tea

This tea is said to help liver and kidney conditions and stomach upsets. It is also used as a general tonic.

300 ml ($\frac{1}{2}$ pint/$1\frac{1}{4}$ cups) boiling water
15 ml (1 tbsp) juniper berries, crushed in a mortar

Pour the boiling water over the crushed berries in a teapot. Cover and infuse for 10 minutes. Strain. Sweeten with honey.
Makes 300 ml ($\frac{1}{2}$ pint/$1\frac{1}{4}$ cups)

Bilberry or Blueberry Tea

Bilberry tea is said in country medicine to be good for stomach upsets. Dried blueberries could be used instead. (See left for how to dry berries.)

15 ml (1 tbsp) dried bilberries or blueberries
1.1 litres (2 pints/5 cups) boiling water

Soak the dried bilberries or blueberries for a few hours. Drain and put into a teapot. Pour the boiling water over them. Cover and infuse for 10 minutes. Strain.
Makes 1.1 litres (2 pints/5 cups)

Rosehip Tea

This is an excellent tea for daily use. Pick the rosehips in late autumn.

30 ml (2 tbsp/3 tbsp) rosehips
(pods and pips in balanced proportion)
1.7 litres (3 pints/$7\frac{1}{2}$ cups) water

Pick the tops and tails off the rosehips. Dry carefully so that they retain their red colour.

Soak the dried rosehips in water in a small container for 12 hours. Bring the water to the boil in an enamel or other non-metal pan. Add the rosehips and simmer gently for 30–40 minutes. Strain. Sweeten with honey, if liked.
Makes about 1.4 litres ($2\frac{1}{2}$ pints/6 cups)

AUTUMN BERRIES AND LATE ROSES

The fruits of autumn are to be enjoyed not only for the wines, drinks and other culinary uses they can be put to, but also purely and simply for their loveliness. Wander along the lanes on a misty autumn day, and you can collect a basket full of berried branches (take your secateurs with you!) with which to make a memorable arrangement. There are the rosehips, scarlet and elegant; dark red haws and perhaps a stem of late elderberries; the first sloes, mysterious blue; and some coral-pink euonymus, which will ripen to reveal its bright seeds inside. Blackberry, with its sculptural leaves, even now has a few red, unripe berries clinging tenaciously to life.

When you get home, recut the stems, remove any berries that would be submerged and immediately put the sprays into water in a large jug or similar container. A big, old-fashioned kettle would look stunning filled with an arrangement of berries. Place it strategically where it can be seen in its full glory, and the mood and beauty of the autumn season will fill the room.

You can make the most of the rich crop of

FENNEL TEA
(PAGE 138) WITH
COB NUT
(FILBERT)
COOKIES
(PAGE 78) AND
WALNUT
COOKIES
(PAGE 87)

ornamental berries in the garden, too. A pre-dominantly red arrangement can be made with berberis, cotoneaster and viburnum, for example, styled dramatically, and put into an eye-catching container. Some golden-yellows – pyracantha for instance – offer brilliant contrast to the reds, and look stunning alongside the scarlet of butcher's broom. The sombre black of privet and dogwood can be added to tone down such an arrangement. Punctuate the berried branches with sprays of coloured leaves, filling out the arrangement with the subtle hues of the turning year and bringing the glory of autumn's colours into your home.

If you keep the water in the container fresh, this arrangement should last for several days or even a week. The cooler the conditions, the longer-lasting the display. An occasional mist-spray with water helps counteract shrivelling. You will probably have to replace the autumnal-coloured foliage with fresh, because once leaves turn colour, their ability to take up water is impaired and they quickly wilt or drop.

BERRIES AND FRUITS FOR COLLECTING
Barberry (Berberis)
Blackberry (Rubus)
Butcher's broom (Ruscus)
Climbing bittersweet (Celastrus)
Cotoneaster
Crab apple (Malus)
Dogwood (Cornus)
Elderberry (Sambucus)
Firethorn (Pyracantha)
Guelder rose (*Viburnum opulus*)
Hawthorn (Crataegus)
Ivy (Hedera)
Privet (Ligustrum)
Rosehips (Rosa)
Rowan (*Sorbus aucuparia*)
Snowberry (Symphoricarpos)
Spindle (Euonymus)
Stinking iris (*I. foetidissima*)
Viburnum
Whitebeam (*Sorbus aria*)

Berries can be preserved in glycerine using the same method as for foliage (see page 109), then sprayed with lacquer hair spray.

On a smaller scale, pick a few late roses, and arrange them simply in a delicate vase with some wild rosehips and a spray or two of dried oats. That's all: the loveliness lies in its simplicity.

You can also preserve late-flowering roses to give you pleasure right through the winter. Tight buds of long-stemmed varieties can be hung upside-down and air-dried, after a few of the leaves at the base are removed. Sprays of small-flowered roses, such as 'The Fairy', can also be treated in this way. For short-stemmed roses, thread the stems through a rack made from 5 cm (2 inch) wire netting; rest the heads on the frame covered with a layer of tissue paper to protect the bottom flower petals from being bruised.

To preserve the beauty of large roses in full flower, you must use a desiccant. Desiccants are powdery or granular substances, such as 'silver sand' or silica gel, which absorb the moisture from the flowers but allow them to retain their natural colour and form.

Preserving Roses: the Sand Method

Use fine white 'silver sand', which you can obtain from garden centres and hardware stores. You can use this repeatedly, so long as you sieve out any particles of plant material after each use. Beach and river sand can also be used but must be washed in several changes of water, until all traces of debris and salt are removed, and then thoroughly dried.

Alternatively, you can use silica gel, which is available from chemists, or drugstores, and is made up of water-absorbent crystals. The crystals can be ground, or crushed with a rolling pin, into a powder, which is easier to use and more effective. Silica gel is sometimes treated so that it is blue when dry and pink when moist. Other brands are sold with special paper or devices for measuring the moisture content. Silica gel is very expensive, but can be dried and re-used indefinitely. It takes much less time – usually a matter of days – than sand.

The only other equipment needed is an airtight container, such as a tin or plastic box. Get all your materials together and ready before picking the roses, so as little time as possible elapses between picking and preserving. To check that the sand itself is completely dry, put a few treated silica gel crystals into the sand; if they go pink, the sand is moist and the flowers will rot. The remedy is to put the sand into a low oven at 150°C/300°F/mark 2 until the silica gel crystals turn blue.

Pick roses when half to three-quarters open and absolutely dry. Fully open roses almost always shatter in desiccant. Moisture causes brown spots to appear on the petals, and if the centre of the flower is damp it may rot and cause the petals to fall off. To check for dryness, sprinkle the flowers carefully with sand. If the sand does not adhere anywhere, you may proceed.

Roses preserved on their own stems tend to flop at the neck. To prevent this, cut the stems back to 3.5 cm (1½ inches), and push a medium

gauge florists' wire up the centre; as the stem shrinks, it will grip the wire. A wire 5 cm (2 inches) long is best, for ease of handling and to fit into the container. Once the roses are preserved, you can add length to the stems, using additional stub wire.

Put a 2.5 cm (1 inch) layer of sand in the container. Place the roses, right way up, carefully on the sand, with the petals in a natural position and not touching each other. To start with, only put one layer of flowers in a container; as you become more experienced, you can put two or more layers of flowers in a deep container.

Embed the roses gently into the sand, so they are secure and stable. Trickle the sand between all the petals until the air spaces are completely filled, using a fine paintbrush to get the sand into every crevice. Cover with 1 cm ($\frac{1}{2}$ inch) sand, then place the covered container in a dry, warm place – near a radiator or in an airing cupboard, for instance. Drying in sand is a slow process and can take a month or more. The

method is much the same for silica gel, but roses takes 2–3 days to dry.

When the approximate drying time is up, gently scrape away the desiccant and lift out one flower. If it feels dry and crisp, tip the sand gently out of the box through your fingers, catching each rose in turn. Be very careful because the flowers are brittle and will break easily. Remove any sand remaining on the petals with a small paintbrush.

Store the dried flowers by sticking them into florists' foam, in an airtight box. Ideally, sprinkle a few grains of silica gel into the box, to absorb any moisture still in the flowers or in the container. Keep the dried flowers in a dry, dust-free place.

Try drying chrysanthemums in this way, too – they make exceptionally lovely arrangements during the winter months. Handle them with care, however, as they shatter easily, especially the large-flowered varieties; you may have to glue the petals to the central disc.

A Winter Posy

A delicate and subtly coloured posy makes an original table decoration for the winter, and you can make one using the different techniques for drying and preserving. From the air-dried flowers, select small sprays of eryngium, lavender, wild carrot and xeranthemum. Add a few wired roses preserved in sand, and some fine grasses. Arrange them in an informal posy, and surround with skeletonized leaves to make a lacy collar. Tie the bunch spirally with florists' wire, so that it is held firmly, and put into a small porcelain vase or a little jug.

Chinese Lanterns

Physalis, the well-loved Chinese lantern, makes a striking arrangement used on its own in an eyecatching container, placed on a table with a pumpkin or some ornamental gourds.

An interesting and original way to treat physalis is to cut the gauzy, delicate calyx down the five seams that enclose the berry, and open them out into a star shape. Place these bright stars on a pretty plate or in a shallow glass bowl, and put it in a sunny spot by a window.

The Fruits of Autumn

Another of the many brightly coloured fruits of the autumn season is the golden bullace. It too is at its prime during these mellow autumn days. Golden bullaces make delectable fruit pies, and also a memorable vinegar which takes on the flavour and lushness of the fruit – it is wonderful in winter salad dressings. This takes its place as one of a variety of sauces and vinegars on the larder shelf, as the fruits of the season continue to be harvested.

CHAPTER FOUR

Vinegars and Sauces for the Larder

The country harvest draws to its close as autumn merges into winter. Euonymus berries, bright coral-pink, illumine the bare, dun-coloured hedge. An occasional leaf drifts quietly on to the numb earth. The last of the hawthorn berries and rose-hips hang singly on bare twigs. In an after-noon sun that slants its pale light through the still day, a November walk is crisp and cold. The distant honking of migra-ting geese in long-necked flight formation lingers over the quietening land. The leaves underfoot are brittle. They have lost their brightness and faded to earth colours against the wet, limp grass.

Silver light struggles through a faint mist. Twigs stand out against the pale sky like sculpted shapes. The occasional robin forages for food. A lethargic sun, heavy and swollen, travels low in the sky as silence cloaks the land. By now the garden is cut down to the ground, the dead refuse burned on the last bonfire, neatly tidied for the winter's sleep. Tools of the gardener's trade are put to rest along the potting shed wall, where the pale evening sun casts long shadows.

And now the larder shelf is full. Rows of multicoloured jars stand gleam-ing in the cupboard, full of autumn's bounty and the tastes of the season. Jams for winter breakfasts, jellies to grace the great winter festival tables. Spicy chut-neys to warm the stomach and to add variety to simple snacks of bread and cheese. Gleaming conserves of fruit for the dessert course, or to give away as gifts. All these have the personal touch, the integrity of living in tune with the seasons of the year. They are in them-selves a celebration of the country harvest.

The freezer is now stocked with breads and cakes and cookies, a reminder in the bleak months of winter of the lusciousness and distinctive flavours of autumn's produce. Bottles of sauces and vinegars stand ready for use, and the drinks cupboard has its original additions, too. As the preserving pan is put away for another year, a sense of deep satisfaction comes from the fulfilment of this task. The work is done: in the grey weeks ahead, family and friends can enjoy the fruits of these seasonal labours.

November nears its end. The inevi-tability of winter becomes apparent. Hard frosts bind the silent dawn, numbing the hard earth. The first snows fall, morning mists turn to thick fog. Nature sleeps, its annual task achieved, the stirrings of spring as yet unimagined. Defiant of the frost, one last white rose remains on its bare shrub in the garden.

ELDERBERRY VINEGAR (PAGE 153) AND BLACKBERRY VINEGAR (PAGE 153)

Spiced Wild Plum Vinegar

Bullaces impart a fruity tang to a spiced vinegar and leave a trace of their golden colour, too. You can also make this recipe using damsons, in which case the vinegar turns purple. The result, fresh-tasting and spicy, makes a wonderful ingredient for winter salad dressings.

450 g (1 lb) wild plums (bullaces or damsons), halved and stoned

For the spiced vinegar

50 g (2 oz) whole mixed spices, such as cinnamon stick, mace, cloves, allspice, peppercorns, fresh root ginger, mustard seeds etc

1.1 litres (2 pints/5 cups) vinegar

To make the spiced vinegar, tie the spices in a muslin (cheesecloth) bag and put into a pan with the vinegar. Heat gently to just below simmering point and remove from the heat. Cover and leave to cool for 2 hours. Decant into a large jar, still with the spices, and leave for 2 weeks to marinate.

Put the bullaces or damsons into a wide-necked bottle. Cover with the strained vinegar and seal the bottle. Shake daily for 1 week, then leave for 3 weeks before using.

Makes 1.4 litres (2½ pints/6¼ cups)

Thus harvest ends its busy reign
And leaves the fields their peace again
Where autumns shadows idly muse
And tinge the trees with many hues

John Clare: 'The Shepherd's Calendar'

Damson and Basil Sauce

Every summer I grow basil in a row of pots on my kitchen windowsill, where it flourishes. By the end of September or early October, they are just about at the end of their cycle, so I use the last of the crop for this lovely sauce. The distinctively autumnal taste of damson marries beautifully with basil, and the sauce is excellent with roast poultry.

15 g (½ oz) fresh root ginger
2 kg (4½ lb) damsons, stoned and chopped
225 g (8 oz/2 cups) onions, skinned and chopped
100 g (4 oz/⅔ cup) currants
15 g (½ oz/⅛ cup) whole allspice
7 g (¼ oz) dried chillies
7 g (¼ oz) mustard seeds
600 ml (1 pint/2½ cups) white vinegar
225 g (8 oz/1 cup) granulated sugar
25 g (1 oz/2 tbsp) salt
1 large bunch basil, chopped

Bruise the ginger by tapping with a meat hammer or rolling pin to separate the fibres. Put the damsons and onions into a pan with the currants, spices and half of the vinegar. Bring to the boil and simmer for 30 minutes.

Rub the pulp through a sieve and return to the cleaned pan. Add the sugar, salt and remaining vinegar. Bring back to the boil and simmer for 45 minutes until thick and creamy.

Stir the chopped basil into the sauce and leave to cool a little. Pour the sauce into warm, clean jars and cover. Seal.

Makes about 1 litre (1¾ pints/4¼ cups)

Legend has it that basil got its name from the basilisk, a fabled king of serpents that was hatched by a snake from the egg of a cock. Only a weasel was cunning enough to take it on in combat. This he did by eating the herb rue, which gave him such strength that he attacked and killed the monster. From then on it was said that basil and rue would not flourish in the same garden.

Verjuice

This is an ancient traditional English recipe for a kind of cider, which is so sharp that it came to be used as a fermented vinegar rather than a drink. It gets its name from *vert jus*, the sour juice of unripe fruit – the French have also used the juice of unripe grapes in the past. Verjuice makes a really interesting addition to the larder shelf, so when crab apples are abundant it is worth a try.

The original version does not include sugar, but I have found that adding a little sugar makes it nicer.

crab apples

sugar, to taste (optional)

Pick ripe crab apples and put them into a very large bowl. Leave them heaped up until they begin to sweat and ferment. Remove any stalks and rotten parts, then mash the rest of the fruit. Strain through a jelly bag or linen cloth. If liked, add a little sugar, to taste. Bottle the resulting liquid and leave for a month before using as a substitute for vinegar.

Apple Sauce

Apple sauce is an ideal way to use up the annual crop of apples, which are almost always super-abundant. It is worth making large quantities since it freezes very well, and can be used up all through the winter and spring. Try varying the recipe using spices. A touch of ground cinnamon or cloves makes a vast difference. Or add some dill seeds to one batch – it makes a delectable apple pie.

1.8 kg (4 lb) Bramley or other cooking (tart green) apples, peeled, cored and chopped

60 ml (4 tbsp/⅓ cup) granulated sugar

grated rind of 2 lemons

grated rind of 2 oranges

juice of 1 orange

Put the apples into a heavy pan with a little water. Cook over a gentle heat until soft and mushy. Mash to a smooth pulp.

Add the sugar, grated rinds and orange juice and continue to cook, stirring, until the sauce is smooth and the sugar has dissolved.

Makes 1 litre (1¾ pints/4¼ cups)

Cranberry and Apple Sauce

A variation on simple cranberry sauce, this makes a tasty alternative to offer up on the Christmas table, alongside all the other trimmings.

250 g (8 oz/2 cups) cranberries
350 g (12 oz/3 cups) apples, peeled,
cored and sliced
30 ml (2 tbsp/3 tbsp) fresh orange juice
225 g (8 oz/1 cup) soft brown sugar
5 ml (1 tsp) ground mixed spice
grated rind of 1 orange

Put all the ingredients into a pan and cook over a medium heat, stirring from time to time, for 15 minutes. Add a little water to thin to the required consistency.
Makes 700 g (1½ lb)

Cranberry Sauce

The traditional Thanksgiving or Christmas turkey would not be the same without cranberry sauce, which makes the perfect complement for it. There is no doubt that the home-made variety is in a different league from any shop-bought brand. The sauce is very simple to make.

175 g (6 oz/1½ cups) cranberries
water or orange juice
sugar

Put the cranberries into a small pan and add water to just cover them. Simmer gently for about 4 minutes until the berries burst.

Strain off half of the liquid and weigh the remainder. Add half the weight of sugar, stir in and dissolve.
Serves 4–6

Winter Relish

This relish is a wonderful addition to a salad table and also goes well with roast chicken.

450 g (1 lb) cooking apples (tart green apples), peeled, cored and chopped
350 g (12 oz/3 cups) onions, skinned and chopped
700 g (1½ lb) blackberries, hulled
700 g (1½ lb) elderberries, stripped off their stalks
600 ml (1 pint/2½ cups) white vinegar
5 ml (1 tsp) ground allspice
5 ml (1 tsp) ground cinnamon
30 ml (2 tbsp) salt
6 cloves
6 peppercorns
450 g (1 lb/2 cups) granulated sugar

Place the apples, onions, blackberries and elderberries in a pan with the vinegar and spices. Bring to the boil and simmer for 15–20 minutes.

Rub through a nylon sieve. Return the pulp to the cleaned pan. Add the sugar and stir over a gentle heat until dissolved. Bring back to the boil and boil rapidly for about 20–30 minutes until thickened. Pour the relish into warm, clean jars and cover. Seal.

Makes about 2 kg (4½ lb)

Elderberry Catsup

Based on an old English country recipe, this 'catsup', or ketchup, is presumably the forerunner of the ubiquitous 'brown' sauce found next to the salt and pepper on many a table. Elderberry catsup is rich, fruity and full of autumnal flavour. An interesting addition to the larder.

450 ml ($\frac{3}{4}$ pint/2 cups) malt vinegar
450 g (1 lb) ripe elderberries, stripped off their stalks
4 shallots, skinned and sliced
2.5 ml ($\frac{1}{2}$ tsp) salt
1 slice fresh root ginger
1 blade of mace
40 peppercorns
12 cloves

Boil the vinegar and pour over the elderberries in a glazed earthenware dish. Stand, covered, in the oven at 110°C/225°F/mark $\frac{1}{4}$ overnight. Strain.

Put the liquid into a pan with the shallots, salt and spices, then boil for 10 minutes. Leave to cool.

When cold, bottle and store for at least 1 year – it is said to be at its best after 7 years! Strain before using.

Makes 750 ml ($1\frac{1}{4}$ pints/3 cups)

Elderberry Vinegar

A powerful vinegar, very dark in colour and extraordinarily strong in its elderberry flavour. This vinegar adds a distinctive touch of autumn to sauces and dressings, and keeps indefinitely.

700 g (1½ lb) elderberries
600 ml (1 pint/2½ cups) white vinegar
450 g (1 lb/2 cups) granulated sugar

Cover the elderberries generously with water in a pan and simmer for 20 minutes, partially covered. Cover and leave until cold.

Strain off the juice into a pan – there will be about 300 ml (½ pint/1¼ cups). Add the vinegar and sugar and stir well over a gentle heat. Bring to the boil and simmer for 5–10 minutes until the liquid becomes syrupy and clings to the spoon. Pour into bottles and seal.
Makes 1.1 litres (2 pints/5 cups)

The elder tree is the dwelling-place of the elder-mother, who will avenge any injury done to the tree. Elder is a tree of ill-omen, and countrymen used to raise their caps to it as they walked past. A tree of shame, it was used for hanging criminals. One tradition says that Judas hanged himself from an elder.

Blackberry Vinegar

This dark red, slightly sweet vinegar is beautifully spicy and full of the flavour of ripe blackberries. It is delicious in salad dressings. Use it instead of wine vinegar either in a vinaigrette or mixed with soy sauce and a little garlic to make an Oriental-style dressing.

20 ml (4 tsp) cloves
20 ml (4 tsp) allspice berries
two 7.5 cm (3 inch) cinnamon sticks
600 ml (1 pint/2½ cups) white vinegar
900 g (2 lb/4 cups) granulated sugar
900 g (2 lb) blackberries, hulled

Tie the spices in a muslin (cheesecloth) bag. Place in a pan with the vinegar and sugar. Dissolve the sugar over a gentle heat, then bring to the boil and simmer for 5 minutes. Add the blackberries and simmer for a further 10 minutes.

Leave to cool completely, then strain into clean bottles and seal.
Makes 1.1 litres (2 pints/5 cups)

Raspberry Vinegar

Whatever else I make with the summer or autumn harvest of raspberries, Raspberry Vinegar is an annual 'must'. I make enough to last me through the year, so that I always have a supply in the larder. I use it all the time in salad dressings, improvising with Chinese flavours like ginger and garlic, soy sauce and sesame oil. The various combinations make stunning Oriental dressings for all types of salads.

700 g (1½ lb) raspberries
1.1 litres (2 pints/5 cups) malt vinegar
900 g (2 lb/4 cups) granulated sugar

Put the raspberries with water to cover in a pan and simmer for 30 minutes, partially covered. Strain off the juice into a pan – there will be about 1.1 litres (2 pints/5 cups).

Add the vinegar and sugar and stir well over a gentle heat. Bring to the boil and simmer for 5–10 minutes until the liquid becomes syrupy and clings to the spoon. Pour into bottles and cork well.
Makes 1.7 litres (3 pints/7½ cups)

To dream of passing through bramble unhurt means that you will triumph over your enemies.

Raspberry Sauce

Otherwise known as Melba sauce – after Dame Nellie Melba, who was so fond of it – a simple purée of raspberries makes one of the best dessert sauces in the world. It freezes extremely well, so if you take advantage of fresh raspberries at the height of their season, you can treat yourself to this luxury at any time of the year.

raspberries, hulled
sugar
lemon juice

Simply blend raspberries in a food processor or blender with a little sugar to taste. Add a little lemon juice to sharpen the flavour. If freezing the sauce, put into small containers.

Tomato Coulis

This sauce can be used right through the winter as it freezes very well.

30 ml (2 tbsp/3 tbsp) olive oil
100 g (4 oz/1 cup) onion, skinned and finely chopped
10 ml (2 tsp) plain (all-purpose) flour
1.4 kg (3 lb) ripe tomatoes, skinned and chopped
2 garlic cloves, skinned and crushed
bouquet garni, tied in a muslin (cheesecloth) bag
2.5 cm (1 inch) piece of orange rind
salt, to taste

Soften the onion in the oil for 10 minutes. Stir in the flour and cook gently for 3 minutes. Stir in the remaining ingredients.

Cover the pan so that the tomatoes render their juices, then uncover and cook for a further 20 minutes, stirring from time to time. Add more water if necessary to prevent burning. The final sauce should be thick, not watery. Remove the bag of herbs. Put into 225 g (8 oz) containers. Makes about 900 ml (1½ pints/1 quart)

Ripe Tomato Sauce

This fresh tomato sauce is spiked with a little cayenne and some tarragon vinegar.

5.5 kg (12 lb) ripe tomatoes, sliced
40 g (1½ oz/3 tbsp) salt
pinch of cayenne
pinch of paprika
450 g (1 lb/2 cups) granulated sugar
600 ml (1 pint/2½ cups) spiced vinegar (see page 148)
45 ml (3 tbsp/4 tbsp) tarragon vinegar

Put the tomatoes into a pan and cook gently until the skins detach. Rub the pulp through a sieve and return to the cleaned pan.

Add the salt, cayenne and paprika and cook until the mixture begins to thicken. Add the sugar and flavoured vinegars and cook gently until creamy. Pour the sauce into warm, clean sauce bottles and cover. Seal. Suitable for freezing. Makes about 1.7 litres (3 pints/7½ cups)

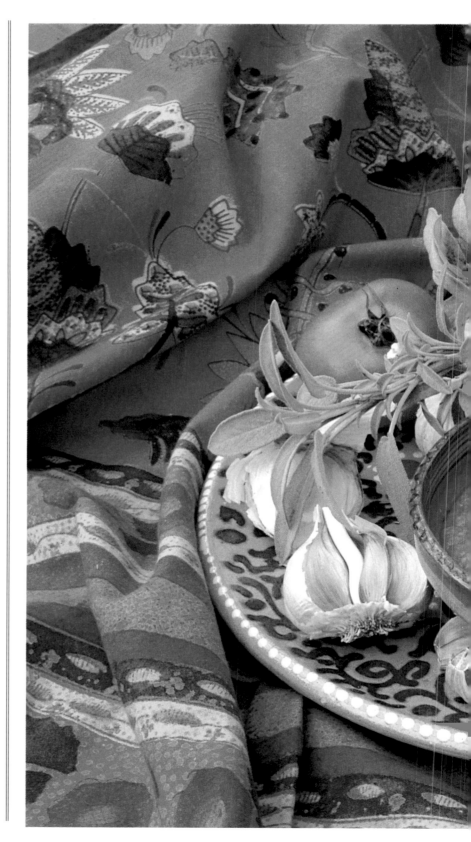

TOMATO COULIS
(PAGE 154)

Tomato Ketchup

There can be no comparison between this home-made ketchup and the shop-bought variety. The flavour of orange and the peppery spices highlight the freshness of the tomatoes.

2.7 kg (6 lb) tomatoes, skinned and chopped
1 onion, skinned and chopped
3 garlic cloves, skinned and chopped
5 ml (1 tsp) paprika
5 ml (1 tsp) cayenne
juice of 1 orange
5 ml (1 tsp) salt
225 g (8 oz/1 cup) granulated sugar
300 ml ($\frac{1}{2}$ pint/$1\frac{1}{4}$ cups) white vinegar

Put the tomatoes into a preserving pan with the onion and garlic. Cook slowly until the onion is soft and the tomatoes are pulpy. Add all the other ingredients and continue to cook until the mixture has a thick, creamy consistency. Sieve or purée in a blender.

Pour the hot ketchup into warm, clean bottles and cover. Seal. Once opened, the ketchup should be stored in the refrigerator and used up as quickly as possible.
Makes about 2.3 litres (4 pints/$2\frac{1}{2}$ quarts)

Tomato Relish

As their leaves die back in early autumn, tomato vines hang heavy with fruit. There is nothing quite like the flavour of a newly picked tomato. You can preserve this flavour for later in the year, as a reminder of the fading summer.

450 g (1 lb) cucumber or marrow (zucchini or squash), peeled, seeded and diced
1.4 kg (3 lb) tomatoes, skinned and chopped
50 g (2 oz/$\frac{1}{4}$ cup) salt
2 garlic cloves, skinned and finely chopped
1 large red pepper, seeded and roughly chopped
450 ml ($\frac{3}{4}$ pint/2 cups) white vinegar
15 ml (1 tbsp) dry mustard
2.5 ml ($\frac{1}{2}$ tsp) ground allspice
2.5 ml ($\frac{1}{2}$ tsp) mustard seeds

Layer the cucumber or marrow (zucchini or squash) with the tomatoes in a bowl, sprinkling each layer with salt. Cover and leave to stand overnight.

Strain off the liquid and rinse the vegetables well. Place in a large pan with the garlic and red pepper. Blend the vinegar with the dry ingredients, stir into the pan and bring slowly to the boil. Simmer gently for about 1 hour, stirring occasionally, until the mixture is soft.

Spoon the relish into warm, clean jars and cover. Seal immediately. Store for 3–4 months before use.
Makes about 1.4 kg (3 lb)

Walnut Sauce

Kicking through damp, multicoloured leaves searching for nuts under the walnut tree is one of autumn's many pleasures. I keep a handful or two of walnuts aside to make this wonderful creamy sauce, in which the nutty, garlicky flavour is perfectly balanced by the flavour of the parsley. It is delectable as a sauce for pasta, and lovely with chicken.

50 g (2 oz/$\frac{1}{2}$ cup) walnuts, finely ground
1 large bunch parsley, chopped
25 g (1 oz/$\frac{1}{2}$ cup) fresh wholewheat breadcrumbs
olive oil
2 garlic cloves, skinned and finely chopped
salt and pepper
150 ml ($\frac{1}{4}$ pint/$\frac{2}{3}$ cup) double (heavy) cream

Mix the walnuts and parsley in a bowl. Add the breadcrumbs. Gradually stir in the olive oil until it reaches the consistency of thick cream.

Season to taste with the garlic and salt and pepper. Thin with the cream. Serve chilled.
Serves 3–4

Walnuts are said to be lucky in marriage, being a symbol of regeneration. In the wedding ceremonies of ancient Rome, the bride and bridegroom threw walnuts to the children among the wedding guests, symbolizing their leave-taking of childish amusements.

Walnut Ketchup

This country recipe dates back many centuries, when home-made sauces were more or less necessary to mask the taste of an unending winter diet of salted meat. The ketchup matures to an extraordinary flavour.

25 green walnuts
2 onions, skinned and chopped
2 garlic cloves, skinned and chopped
15 g ($\frac{1}{2}$ oz/1 tbsp) salt
600 ml (1 pint/2$\frac{1}{2}$ cups) malt vinegar

4 cloves
2 blades of mace
8 peppercorns

Chop the nuts and pound them in a mortar until well crushed. Mix the onions and garlic with the nuts in a bowl. Add the salt and vinegar so that the nuts are well covered. Leave for 10 days, stirring daily.

Strain off the liquid into a pan. Add the spices and boil for 20 minutes. Strain and pour into bottles.

Makes 600 ml (1 pint/2$\frac{1}{2}$ cups)

The name *basil* comes from the Greek meaning a king. The king of herbs, it was also used as a royal unguent or medicine in ancient times.

Walnut Garlic Sauce

The inspiration for this sauce is the classic Greek dish, *skordalia*, a rustic dip which is traditionally eaten with deep-fried vegetables, fish or chicken. You can use it as a dip for crudités, too, and it goes especially well with the first crisp white celery of the season.

2 medium slices day-old bread, crusts removed
15–30 ml (1–2 tbsp) water
100 g (4 oz/1 cup) walnuts, finely ground
4 garlic cloves, skinned and crushed
olive oil
salt, to taste

Soak the bread in the water for 1 minute, then squeeze it dry. Purée the bread, walnuts and garlic in a food processor or grinder.

Mix in olive oil, drop by drop as for mayonnaise, until it reaches the consistency required. Season to taste with salt.

Serves 3–4

Pesto

I use basil copiously through the summer in salads and sauces. At times when it grows faster than I can use it, I make Pesto to use through the weeks ahead. I usually serve it on fresh pasta, a classic and unbeatable combination.

1 large bunch fresh basil leaves
2 large garlic cloves, skinned and crushed
75 g (3 oz/¾ cup) pine nuts
150 ml (¼ pint/⅔ cup) olive oil
50 g (2 oz/½ cup) Parmesan, finely grated
salt (optional)
lemon juice

Purée the basil, garlic, nuts and olive oil in a blender to a smooth paste, adding more olive oil if necessary. Stir in the grated Parmesan. Season to taste with salt or lemon juice or both.

Put the sauce into a clean screw-top jar. Pesto will keep in the refrigerator for several weeks.

Makes 450 g (1 lb)

MINT VINEGAR
(THIS PAGE)

Wayward women in Roman times made a mint paste with honey to disguise the scent on their breath after drinking wine, which was forbidden by law and punishable by death.

Mint Vinegar

A clump of mint grows near my garden gate, and every time I brush past it on those damp, misty mornings that herald the autumn, I am amazed by its potent scent. This vinegar takes pride of place among my salad dressing collection. It tastes wonderful, and looks very pretty standing on the windowsill in the last of the autumn sunshine, while the leaves are steeping.

fresh mint sprigs
white vinegar

Gather the mint on a sunny morning if possible, then wash and dry it. To scald the vinegar, bring it to just below boiling point, then leave to cool.

Put 4–5 sprigs of mint into each 600 ml (1 pint/2½ cup) bottle, then pour the vinegar over them through a funnel. Seal the bottle. Leave to stand on a sunny windowsill for 2–3 weeks until the vinegar takes on the flavour of the mint. Remove to the larder shelf ready for use.

Lavender Vinegar

In my front garden I planted an English lavender next to an old rose, and they flourish in each other's company. Each year the lavender puts out a mass of beautifully scented flowerheads, which I harvest for pot-pourri and also add to the scented bags that I use in clothes drawers. I always reserve a bunch for lavender vinegar, to which it gives its inimitable scent and a fragrant, flowery flavour. This vinegar is also delightfully different in a vinaigrette.

6 sprigs dried lavender
450 ml (¾ pint/2 cups) white wine vinegar

Put the lavender sprigs into a bottle with the wine vinegar.

Seal the top and leave on a sunny windowsill for 2–3 weeks to draw out the fragrance of the lavender into the vinegar. It is then ready for the larder shelf.

Makes 450 ml (¾ pint/2 cups)

LATE HERBS, TREE CONES AND NUTS

Jars and bottles, filled with the rich variety of autumn's produce, stand on the larder shelf ready for the winter: jams and jellies, chutneys and conserves, drinks and cordials, sauces and vinegars. November drifts into December, and Christmas looms into sight.

As well as giving away attractively packaged jars of autumnal goodies as gifts, you can also make cards, presents and house-decorations the natural way, using many of the plants growing all around. Late-picked flowers and leaves can be pressed for greetings cards, and wreaths and table decorations can be made using ripened wheat or wild oats, tree cones and seeds such as acorns and beech-mast.

The result is a far cry from glitz. Christmas can look like the celebration of winter that it originally was, with natural forms and colours decorating the house. There is much beauty in gifts which are hand-made and which use plants that grow very commonly all around.

Pressing Late Flowers and Herbs

The art of pressing flowers goes way back in time – probably to the time when medical herbalists started to make their *herbaria* by pressing samples of leaves and flowers on a flat surface and leaving them under a heavy weight until dry. Books have long been used for pressing flowers, and they still remain the simplest and most commonly used method. Sandwiching the flowers to be pressed between sheets of blotting paper speeds the drying process and protects the flowers and book.

You can also press flowers and leaves in a flower-press; small ones are widely available through craft shops, or you can quite easily make one yourself. The drying process is much quicker in a flower press than in a book, and the pressed flowers themselves are of better quality.

Start with single, simple flowers and leaves, and then go on to more complex ones. Try to include buds as well as fully open flowers, but bisect thick buds before pressing, cutting them cleanly down the centre. Flowers with trumpet shapes, many layers of petals or long spurs are difficult to press; they usually have to be taken apart for pressing, then reconstructed once dried. Thick-stemmed flowers can have the stamens cut back, or can be pressed with special padding foam over the petals, creating two-tiered pressure. Avoid damaged, fleshy or very thick, three-dimensional plant material – though if you want the colour provided by bulky flowers, you can take them apart and press individual petals.

Some colours are retained better than others; generally, pure, bright hues, especially yellow, are longer-lasting than pastels and subtle shades and tints.

Pick your flowers or leaves on a fine day, and before you press them make sure that they are completely dry. Press flowers and foliage as soon as possible after picking, since if they have withered at all they will emerge crumpled. Before pressing, remove the stems; these can, if wished, be pressed separately. Always press material of the same thickness in a single layer. Varying thicknesses may prevent the thinnest petals and/or leaves from coming into contact with the blotting paper, reducing the pressure on them.

You can place the material close together, but it should not overlap. Cover the flowers or leaves with another layer of paper, inserting a marker recording the type of flowers and foliage and the date pressed. Close the press as instructed by the makers; or close the book carefully and put it under a heavy weight, such as several other thick books or some bricks.

It will take the flowers about 10–14 days to dry, but the longer the material is left in the press, the more the colour is retained. Six months is ideal. Thick material may need several changes of blotting paper during the drying time.

You can add more flowers to the press or book during this time, but take care not to disturb the ones already there. Once they are dry, remove them carefully and store them flat, for example between sheets of blotting paper inserted in the pages of magazines. For tidiness and easy access, aim to prevent large flowers and leaves from curling up. Exposure to bright sunlight, moisture or dust during storage can destroy all your hard work.

LATE FLOWERS AND HERBS
FOR PRESSING
Borage (Borago)
Caryopteris
Catmint (Nepeta)
Chervil (Anthriscus)
Chrysanthemum
Dill (Anethum)
Fennel (Foeniculum)
Fuchsia
Goldenrod (Solidago)
Hardy plumbago (Ceratostigma)
Heather (Calluna, Erica)
Herb Robert (*Geranium robertianum*)
Hydrangea
Japanese anemone (*Anemone hybrida*)
Knotweed (Polygonum)
Michaelmas daisy (Aster)
Mint (Mentha)
Montbretia (Crocosmia)
Pansy (Viola)
Pearl everlasting (Anaphalis)
Rose (Single-flowered species and varieties)
Rose-bay willow herb (Epilobium)
Rue (Ruta)
Sage (Salvia)
Tobacco plant (Nicotiana)

MOUNTING PRESSED FLOWERS
Once you have decided what to make with your pressed flowers and leaves, they may need to be glued to a surface. Clear, liquid, 'photographic' glue is the best bet, since it can be used with precision and does not leave too many marks. Only the smallest possible amount of glue will actually be needed, smeared lightly on to the

back of the flower or leaf. Handle carefully, as it is very fragile.

This process has to be carried out with great care, since glue can mark noticeably, and very easily, and it smudges if corrections have to be made. Let the glue dry for a day. If the articles made are to be used, rather than framed behind glass, they should be coated with natural matt varnish. Greetings cards are best covered with adhesive plastic film.

Ideas for Gifts

Pressed flowers, leaves and ferns can be used to make lovely gifts and cards that have a truly personal touch.

GREETINGS CARDS
Choose softly coloured pastel backgrounds on which to glue pressed flowers and leaves, or skeletonized leaves (see page 113). Handle them carefully with tweezers, and finish the card with adhesive plastic film.

GIFT TAGS
Glue pressed flowers or leaves to small rectangular cards, punching a hole in one end and threading strands of embroidery silk through for the tie. Cover with self-adhesive plastic film.

SMALL GIFTS
Matchboxes and book marks can be made in the same way as gift tags; finish them with a coat of clear varnish or clear film. Calendars, too, can make original and pretty gifts, and children can make them very easily.

CANDLES
You can glue delicate petals or tiny pressed flowerheads, ferns and leaves, around a candle, and coat it with varnish when the glue has dried. These make lovely gifts, or they can be incorporated into Christmas table decorations. They should, however, be used only for decorative purposes; it is not advisable to light them.

Christmas Decorations

You can make beautiful Christmas decorations using dried cones and dried flowers, seedheads and foliage, along with holly and ivy.

For a Christmas ball, cover a ball of florists' foam with Icelandic moss (a type of grey lichen), using florists' staples or pieces of wire shaped like hairpins. Stick into it wired larch cones or pine cones (see page 164), dried cineraria, honesty, hops, small wooden Christmas tree decorations, artificial apples, paper ribbon ties, and pieces of holly or fir.

For a lovely ivy centrepiece, entwine preserved ivy in a circle, wiring it on to a ring of florists' foam and arranging dried flowers, seedheads or cones among the leaves. Stick tall slim candles into the florists' foam, and spray the garland gold or silver.

Mastic, a kind of green clay which does not harden and which can be moulded into any shape, can be used to decorate a candlestick with dried flowers or seedheads. (Be sure to use a tall candle, and then do not allow it to burn low, because the dried flowers are inflammable.)

Roll the required length of mastic into a sausage shape and place it around the candle in order to make a ring that will sit on the rim of the candlestick. Mould it into a perfect circle, then cover it with a little moss. Attach the moss with florists' staples or pieces of wire bent into hairpin shapes. Insert your chosen flowers and leaves carefully, putting them in exactly the right position and facing the right way – they are too brittle to move once in place.

An attractive combination for a candlestick holder could be made with a selection from: artemesia, xeranthemum, tansy, small skeletonized leaves, hop, grasses, physalis, sorrel.

A Festive Wreath

You will need to decide first what materials you want to use in the wreath. Fresh material, such as holly, ivy, fir or blue spruce, is usually fixed to wet florists' foam or a damp moss-covered wire ring. It needs to be hung outside, since it will not last more than about six days in warm, dry air. Although cones and some dried seedheads can be hung outside, dried flowers and delicate seedheads should not be, since they quickly absorb rain and atmospheric moisture.

If you have a porch sheltered from wind and rain, a wreath made from a combination of fresh and dried materials could be hung there. Or, if you plan to hang the wreath outside, use only the less delicate dried materials – such as cones, dried poppy heads, dried lotus heads, or glycerined eucalyptus – along with the fresh materials.

For a dried wreath that will hang indoors or on a sheltered porch, use dry florists' foam. You can buy inexpensive, plastic-backed florists' foam rings, in a variety of sizes, from florists. It is sensible to order them in advance, especially in the weeks before Christmas. Cover the ring with reindeer moss; if hard and inflexible, soak in a

little warm water first. Squeeze it well and fix it to the front and sides of the ring with wires bent into hairpin shapes. Fix a loop of wire for hanging the finished wreath. Once the reindeer moss is absolutely dry, fix wired flowers, seedheads, leaves and cones (see below) on to the base, distributing them evenly. Wire very small flowers together into bundles. Soften the contours with grasses and wild oats, glycerined beech leaves, etc, making sure that the wreath is well covered. Tie a red ribbon into a bow to attach to the bottom of the wreath.

TREE CONES

Unripe cones are closed; they open into their attractive star shapes as they ripen and shed their seeds. You can collect cones at any stage of development, though fir (Abies, Picea) cones shed their scales as well as seeds when ripe, and are best collected when immature. Ripe cones are generally easier to wire than unripe ones. Always dry cones thoroughly before use or storage; remove any pitch or mud first, using detergent and a scrubbing brush. If you want unripe cones to open out, put them near a wood-burner or similar very warm place.

WIRING CONES

Bind a medium- or heavy-gauge stub wire horizontally around a band of scales near the base of the cone, making one side or 'leg' of wire twice as long as the other. Pull the wire hard against the cone, so it slots between two rows of scales, then twist the wire ends together and bend the twisted ends down to form a long stem.

Wire large, heavy cones with two heavy-gauge wires, one horizontally slotted each side of the cone, near the base. Twist the wires together, where they meet at the sides, then bend downwards, and twist to form a single stem.

WIRING LEAVES

For lightweight leaves with stalks attached, simply place a stub wire tight against the stalk and extending a third of the way up the back of the leaf, then bind the stub wire and stalk together using rose wire.

Alternatively, make a long loop of florists' rose wire the length of the leaf stem, with one end as long as required. Place the top of the loop against where the stem joins the leaf, and neatly coil the shorter end of the wire around the longer piece and the stem itself. If there is no stem, use fine-gauge wire to make a small stitch across the midrib, near the base, then bring both wires down and twist together to form a new stalk, incorporating a stub wire if extra length is needed.

WIRING FLOWERS

To wire dried flowers, push a stub wire up through the centre of the flower. Make a hook at the top of the wire and pull it back down so that it is embedded and hidden in the centre of the flower. Twist the lower end of the wire round the top of the stem where it joins the base of the flower head. Leave the rest of the wire as the new stem.

A WINTER CORNUCOPIA

Some ideas for winter arrangements using gold or silver spray paints:

○ A bowl heaped with walnuts, all sprayed gold

○ A jug of honesty and eucalyptus, sprayed silver

○ A dish of different tree cones, sprayed silver and sprinkled with glitter; acorns and beech-mast, left natural, and nuts of all varieties sprayed gold

Autumn's End

Candles lit, the fire flickering. Another rich autumn harvest comes to its end, and winter closes in. The cold earth sleeps until another spring; inside the house the hearth is warm, the larder stocked, the produce of the season reaped and its dried flowers and leaves a sculptural reminder of the dying year. The land is at peace; we have celebrated the country harvest in all its manifestations.

For now the year draws on towards its ending.
Squirrel has hoarded all his nuts, and man,
(Laying for yet another spring his plan,)
Counts over what he has for winter's spending.
Granary's full with heaped and dusty store:
Apples on attic floor
Throughout the house their brackish smell are sending;
The steepled ricks with frost are hoar
In silent yard; the harvest's at its sleeping;
That's slumber now, which once was heyday reaping.

Vita Sackville-West: 'The Land'

INDEX

Page numbers in *italics* indicate captions to photographs.

THE FLOWERS, SEEDHEADS AND FOLIAGE shown in this book include the following: honesty (p. 30); *Solanum jasminoides* and vine leaves (p. 39); dried achillea and *Craspedia globosa* (pp. 46–47); dried hydrangeas, statice, callicarpa and hop (p. 58); chrysanthemums with rowan and snowberry (pp. 74–75); thistledown (p. 93); echinops and Michaelmas daisy (p. 94); teazels (p. 112); decaisnea (p. 128); dahlia with rosehips (pp. 142–143); Chinese lanterns (pp. 144 and 145); clematis seedheads, dried asters and dried fig leaves (p. 163).